CW01090921

Tales of the Unelected

There are so many tensions and emotional conflicts in being a special adviser and Dan Corry takes you into that world through this fascinating collection of stories.

Ed Balls (former special adviser, minister and Shadow Chancellor)

It's an honour to be a special adviser, as I was, but most of what has been written about them is of the sensational type. Here, in all its everyday glory is a real feel of what it is like.

Ayesha Hazarika, former special advisor

Dan Corry's subtle and engrossing short stories are the real thing, a window on the largely hidden lives of the fixers and policymakers of the political world, the notorious advisers. His compelling authority is no accident: reader, he was one.

Robert Peston (Political Editor at ITN)

Tales of the Unelected

Empty Boxes and other short stories from the world of the special adviser

Dan Corry

Bridge House

British Library Cataloguing in Publication Data
A Record of this Publication is available from the British
Library

ISBN 978-1-914199-70-7

This edition published 2024 by Bridge House Publishing
Manchester, England

Cover photo © Dinah Roake

While the stories naturally build on some of my own
experiences and the personalities I worked with, all are
products of my imagination.

Contents

Introduction

I was very lucky to have worked at the heart of the UK Labour government for a prolonged period between 1997 and 2010 as a political special adviser (a "spad"). I worked in various departments for a number of different Secretaries of State including the Treasury and for the Prime Minister in No.10 Downing Street. It is a fascinating, hard and strange job. Some special advisers work mainly on press and presentation – and they have been portrayed in fiction in things like *The Thick of It*. I was more behind the scenes and a policy specialist (I am an economist by profession). I hope that these stories give you the reader a feel of what it is like to work as a spad, what the pressures are and which conflicts emerge when one tries to do it well. And I hope they are a good read! In many ways they bring up universal themes present in many other walks of life.

Arriving as a Special Adviser

The night of the election victory was sweet indeed. Ed had savoured it. God, it was so good to win. It had been long fought for and although most thought they would win, the campaign had been long and tiring and the polls had narrowed near the end.

But that was just the beginning.

Ed had been appointed as special adviser to the Secretary of State in the Industry department the next day and he could not have been more excited or nervous. He took ages that morning trying to work out what to wear.

"Come on, Jane," he said to his wife, "give me a hand in sorting this out." She looked up at him in a mildly interested way. The kids still had to get to school and at five and eight, that took a lot of work, not least since Hannah had lost the art scrapbook she was making, that she was supposed to show to her teacher that morning.

Ed had to look the part – but he wasn't really sure what that was. He put on his brown suit. No that wasn't right – and he didn't need Jane to tell him that. It had been dragged from the back of the wardrobe, and he could only just squeeze into it. The brown was just so wrong, and then Jane noticed a bit of a stain on it anyway. In the end he went for a traditional charcoal suit with a plain red tie... *Well they had just won the election!*

He fumbled over the bag too. The briefcase felt good in his hand and made him feel serious. But as Jane said, it made him look like a Tory. So he tried a couple of backpacks he had, dumping the one that looked a bit like a student out of *The Young Ones* – but which he had used for his last job – in favour of a dull-looking black one. But still, when he arrived at the Department his hands were trembling so he shoved them hard in his trouser pockets.

The wait to be met by a civil servant to take him through the process of getting a security pass seemed to take ages. *Was he really up to this? Could he actually do it? Would they all find him out?*

It was all pretty unexpected. He had worked just a little with the now Secretary of State when the Party was in opposition. But that was a good few years ago. He'd left her to work in a think-tank and assumed the political part of his life was at an end. But he'd come back into the picture during the election campaign, taking leave of absence from his job to help out. And now, here he was.

It was what he had always dreamed of doing, but his stomach was tight. He didn't know how it would all work out, but he knew his life was about to change big time. This was a serious job with big responsibilities. The way he carried himself would have to change, what he could and could not say in public would be different. And there would be tension at home too as the workload would crowd out much of his domestic life. It really was a new adventure and he half wanted it to all go away.

The first few days were a whirlwind. He attended lots of meeting that were aimed at helping his boss. They were a bit about process – how the private office worked, how the diary worked, what Cabinet committee she would be on, how to get things done. And a lot about the policy of the government as the civil service tried to get its head around what this new government, the first for over a decade, was all about.

In a baffling way, civil servants presented them with folder after folder analysing what the new government had said in their manifesto and other documents, speeches and press conferences. And they had prepared papers on how to pursue them, what the options were, what the dangers were.

It was wild.

They had massively over interpreted words and meaning. They had tried to read between the lines and had got it all wrong – not understanding that so much of the craft in the manifesto drafting was finding words that kept all the parts of the Party together. To say you wanted a partnership with the trade unions did not mean you wanted a formal German style agreement – and he laughed out loud when he read that.

Even more crazily they had found out what he – Ed – had written about before and had assumed that some of this was likely to be on the minister's agenda. OK, maybe not totally crazy. But to assume that every idea he had thrown around in his think-tank days was now about to become policy was way off the mark. Even Ed didn't think that would be a good idea.

Ed also had a few one-to-one, private meetings with his boss. Her office was furnished in modern, neat furniture, with white walls and healthy-looking, tall potted plants, It was a far cry from some of the rooms he remembered working in when the Party was in opposition – with stuff crammed in, computer wires trailing everywhere, Blu Tack and Sellotape marks all over the walls, empty coffee cups and plates littering the rooms. Here all seemed in order. The computers all worked, staff cleared up and made things look nice. He supposed regular cleaners came in overnight and he wondered how much they got paid.

"So, how do you think it's going?" he asked Ruth, his boss.

She sighed but smiled. "There is a lot to absorb. An awful lot. It's exciting and there's great responsibility, but at the moment I need to find a way to concentrate on the key things."

"I know," said Ed, "there is so much material that there is a big danger of getting drowned in it all."

They sat in silence for a moment. Ed was taking it all in, sat here in an actual Secretary of State's office. *Wow.*

Then Ruth got up from her desk, her eyes sharp and focussed as she looked at him.

"What I think we need to do is to get them working on what we want. To show the outside world and the civil service machine what it is we – this government – are all about."

"And what you are all about," Ed added quietly.

He agreed strongly. Of course, they could correct some of the misinterpretation of the manifesto that officials had made, and get them working on how to implement the real manifesto promises. But they needed something quicker, faster. More immediate.

"What's in your mind?" he asked.

"I'm not sure, Ed." She stared into her tea cup as though she was about to read the leaves. Then her eyes lit up.

"Something that gets across our approach to the economy. We are not about to nationalise the top 100 companies. But we are not free marketers either. We don't want government taking decisions that the private sector should, but we don't think keeping government out of the way is the right thing either."

Ed smiled. He loved the energy in her voice, the excitement in her eyes. He wanted to help her. She was right. Something like that was needed. But he could not work out what it should be. He stared at the picture on the wall behind her, an abstract painting with great splodges of colour and a big black frame, feeling a bit useless.

It was his boss that took the next step.

"I think it might be something around the manufacturing sector. If we publish something about that then it shows we are not just leaving everything to the market and we are not neutral about which sectors of the economy do or don't do well." She was warming to her subject with an eager tone in her voice. "And it will go down well with our supporters and MPs – and show we meant what we always said."

Ed worked until close to midnight on his notes before being encouraged to leave the building by the security guy doing his rounds. He had missed supper, baths and bedtime stories with his children, although he had rung home for a very brief chat to them all. He had no idea what had happened with Hannah's scrapbook. He felt bad but also exhilarated with the excitement and adrenalin of it all. *I wonder if these people on the Tube going home know what I do.*

Next morning he was up and out of the house before anyone else was awake.

Back in the office, and after placing a photo of his wife and kids on his desk, Ed soon found himself in a meeting room with three of the most powerful civil servants in the department.

They had been called in the previous day by the Secretary of State who had in general terms described what she wanted. And then she had finished with words that made Ed bristle with pride – and fear – "And Ed will lead this work, so I want you to work with him to get me a rough outline of something in the next few days."

It was like being the bull entering the bullring – nervous, anxious and uncertain, but wanting to show an outward sign of bravery and fearlessness.

"So, Ed," said the senior head of the competitiveness section of the department, "if it's OK to call you that – what do you want us to do?"

It was a reasonable question. Ed knew that. But to Ed it also contained menace: "Come on then, boy, show us what you are made of."

It was a tricky moment. Ed knew his stuff in this area. He was a trained economist. He had been a civil servant in the Treasury. He had written about this sort of thing in the past. He knew the academic literature. But still.

These were hardened civil servants who had been round the block a few times. They had seen special advisers – and ministers – come and go. And worse, they had been working for a government of a very different ideology and belief set for at least a decade.

This would be tough. Was he tough enough?

Ed explained what was wanted. He knew his voice was trembling a bit but he pushed on trying to ignore that.

"What we need is a short paper explaining in simple terms why manufacturing is an important sector, where the UK's strengths and weaknesses are, what the problems are, and with four or five crunchy policy ideas to start pointing the way that this government aims to support the sector."

How would the trio respond to this? Would they go straight for the executioner's sword, or play with him to start with, enjoying the cape work?

He feared they were going to savour this. A long, drawn-out torture.

"Thanks, Ed," said Bob Haldren, the most senior of them, sitting confidently with his arms firmly folded. "That's really helpful. Hope it's OK if we ask a few questions so we make sure we have really got this."

"Of course," said Ed, feeling a bit more relaxed.

"So, just to be clear, the Secretary of State – the government – wants to pick out this sector for special attention and make the case for that."

"That's exactly it," said Ed warming to Bob despite his doubts. Maybe this would not be so hard after all.

"We will have a go then, Ed." But there was more.

"It's not that easy. There is a great deal of academic

work – and work we have done ourselves – that suggests that manufacturing just is declining in our country, that there is not that much we can do about it, that this is the market and comparative advantage at work." He was making his case well but it was riling Ed.

But he still had more.

"And lots of evidence too that governments trying to second guess the market can be a mug's game. Look at Concord. Look at British Leyland."

Ed wanted to tell him to fuck off.

We are the masters now, ditch your old views and get with the elected government of the day. He was oh so tempted. But he tried another way.

"I take your point, Bob, and we must not overdo this. But as I am sure you know, a lot of recent analysis by the top economists, especially in the US, are suggesting that while its relative size may be shrinking, its ability to push innovation, to support the service sector is vital. And as you know manufacturing jobs are good jobs and the public knows that."

He did not add that their pre-election polling showed that manufacturing was very popular with the public, who had a romanticised view through the lens of an old black and white film, that somehow the sector could be revived enormously. Half the Parliamentary Party thought that too.

To be fair, Bob took this in his stride. But with that thrust parried, Bob came another way.

"Would the SoS like us to set a target for the percentage of the economy that should be in manufacturing?"

Ed froze.

In truth he had not got a clue. He didn't really know her well enough on this issue. He thought it a daft idea. But would she?

Her former beliefs, on the left of the Party, suggested

she might well like a target, but she seemed to have changed a lot in recent years since he had last worked with her.

If these guys picked up the scent that he did not really speak for his boss, he knew he would be dead meat. Why should they take his steers if the Secretary of State might not agree with them?

It seemed better to be evasive – even if it was an obvious shimmy around the issue – than be caught out. But that sounded just too weak. He had to take a risk.

"No, she would not go for something like that – and nor would the government."

Another thrust had been parried and he was still alive.

The battle carried on though.

"A last thing, Ed," said Bob with a look of concern on his face, "have you spoken to the Treasury about this? They don't usually like sectoral policy like this and you will need to get clearance for this paper from them as well as from the Economic Policy Cabinet Committee."

Oh Christ.

Ed had only a vague idea of how the processes worked.

Did they really have to pass everything they did through the Treasury – and other members of the Cabinet? What a complete pain if they did because he knew that Bob's characterisation of the Treasury was dead right.

But he mustn't sound naïve. Or sound worried.

He played one of his jokers.

"Well, I will talk this through with Elaine, the Chancellor's main adviser. I know her from our think-tank days a long time ago."

That was clearly some sort of bullseye as he saw a look of respect at last flow across Bob's face. *Maybe he will think that I am useful after all.*

Bob and his henchmen left the room, promising they

would put together some sort of draft outline in the next two days so Ed and the Secretary of State could have a look at it.

Ed was exhausted. He only now realised how tense he had been. He staggered through the rest of the day, using coffee to keep his attention from wavering. He took a taxi rather than the Tube to get home a bit faster. But he was again too late to read bedtime stories.

A few days later they were ready to meet with the Secretary of State. Ed got up extra early that morning so he could at least help the children get washed and dressed a bit before he handed them over to Jane. He tried to ask Hannah about the art scrapbook but at that moment she was more interested in sorting out her hair before the rush to school. He felt just a bit crushed but there was no time to dwell on that. As he munched through his muesli and drank his coffee, he skimmed through the draft paper the officials had prepared, propped up against the milk carton. His heart jumped as he realised he had made an error – a rookie error – in letting the draft paper go direct to the SoS and not insisting he have a look at it before that happened.

For the most part though, it seemed fine. A bit dull and in need of sprucing up. And it needed firmer language, some colour and an injection of energy. But Ed was confident they could add that in when it was needed. He was quietly pleased with the outcome – his steers and relations with the team seemed to have worked. He gave an extra big hug to his kids as he took off out of the door.

He said all this to his boss as they had a short, private chat before the full meeting.

"Anything you don't like in it, Ed?"

"Well, there's a bit where they try to imply the sector is all but doomed in the longer run that will need toning down, and a few other bits where the wording needs changing. And it needs livening up a bit. But for a first draft, I think it's going to do what we wanted it to."

The meeting went pretty smoothly.

Bob didn't know the SoS but he was clearly well used to presenting to ministers. Ed could not help admiring the mixture of confidence and deference he showed. Not least as Ed knew that only a few weeks ago, Bob would have taken the idea of a paper dedicated to manufacturing to bits – according to the wishes of his political masters at the time.

Then something came from left field.

"Secretary of State," Bob began, "we could try to put in some kind of target for the percentage of GDP the government would like manufacturing to be. An indicative target to give a feel of what this all might mean. Would that help?"

Ed felt as though he had just received a kick in the stomach. He had let his guard down. This idea had not been in the paper so he had half forgotten about their chat on this issue. Now he remembered. He had been quite clear that his boss would be against this idea. But would she?

And why hadn't he talked to her about this? Too much going on was a poor excuse.

He was sure there was a smirk on Bob's face as he asked that question. He knew it was a test. And he feared that his face gave away the fact that he didn't know what the result would be.

"An interesting idea, Bob," she began, and Ed's eyes tried to look anywhere but towards her or Bob. "What sort of number would you use as the target?"

"Well, that's a good question," said Bob. "We could use the current percentage and say the government will try to stop it going down, but that may sound not very ambitious – although it is!"

Ed realised that he and Bob were arguing the same thing. They were partners. He wanted to boost the argument.

"And the problem," he said, "is that to go for a higher percentage than now is a hostage to fortune given recent trends."

The Secretary of State was silent for a minute. Ed could hear the clock tick. He could feel his own heartbeat. Then Ruth spoke.

"No, I don't think a target is sensible – and anyway we don't need it for our paper to get cut through."

Ed had survived. And he had learned many lessons about doing this job. It was going to be tough, but he was going to manage this. And that evening he made sure he got back home in time to help Hannah finish off her scrapbook.

The Speech

Ian stared at the poster of Tony Blair.

He looked rather messianic and young, hung on the wall over the desk in Ian's small, but functional, office. Ian was in a strange, slightly distant moment as he thought about the day ahead. He had a lot of work: papers to read, memos to write and meetings to attend.

His musings were interrupted by a phone call from Toby's private secretary who asked him to come down the corridor to talk to the Secretary of State. "OK, I'll be right there, just give me a few minutes to finish what I'm doing." But he screwed up his face in frustration after he put the phone down. "Why does he do that so often?" he said to himself. "Doesn't he understand that I have to have my own meetings, and my own diary to really help him do his job properly and really help him out? Does he think I just hang around waiting for his call? And so often I'm not really needed; he just wants me for moral support." But Ian knew it was an accepted hazard of being a special adviser to a minister that you had to be more or less on call all the time. It wasn't a bad price to pay for being able to do a pretty amazing job. And he really liked Toby.

"Ian," the Secretary of State said, looking up from his oversized but plain light-coloured wooden desk. "Ian, I want to make a speech next Thursday."

"That's good news, Toby," replied Ian, and he actually meant it. He liked helping his boss draft a speech.

Some speeches were routine and dull but had to be given. You just had to give a speech at the Chemical Industries Association annual dinner every now and then and do your turn at the North West Chamber of Commerce Annual Conference. Most of these were routine.

The early days of Toby's time at the Business Department

had been a bit agonising on the speech front. After receiving one draft, Toby had moaned a fair bit to Ian.

"Do they really expect me to say all this stuff? It's so stilted."

"Well, I guess they don't really know your 'voice' yet or what you want to talk about." Ian was surprised to hear himself defending the officials quite so much. So he went tougher.

"It's also a fact that most of them don't know the first thing about how to write a speech."

All that had meant that Toby and Ian (especially Ian) had often had to spend large amounts of time trying to carve out a half-decent speech more or less from scratch. And that was a pain.

But that was the routine speeches. For a speech could also be exciting, it was a chance to make an impact and to create new agendas; to let the world know you were alive, worth taking note of.

That always mattered in politics. You needed a bit of recognition, not just from the public and the people who you wanted to vote for you, but from the political classes, the commentators, your political friends and foes. The people that made the weather in the Westminster bubble.

Ian liked that need for a bit of political positioning. Yes, it was a bit of a game but it could move narratives on, explain to the public what your seemingly random initiatives were all about. It challenged you but it made some sense in the world he was working in; and he understood and respected it.

Toby, however, didn't like all that. He was a quiet, old-fashioned guy in the main. Do your job well, make no mistakes, eschew flamboyance, bring in sensible, well-thought-out policies and you will get on. Except, as Ian knew, you probably wouldn't. People who mattered, people in Number 10, would ask themselves when they came up to a Cabinet reshuffle, "What has Toby been doing lately? Is he helping us make the 'weather'? Are we setting the agenda?" And then they might ask a more worrying question: "Would anyone really notice or complain much if we moved or sacked him to make way for an up-and-coming star?"

It was unfair. Toby had clearly achieved much and he was thoughtful about how he did his job. The fact that he had virtually no journalist contacts should not count against him in a decent world. But politics was a more complex game than that.

All that might be – was – primarily Toby's business. However, the consequences of Toby getting his P45 were severe for Ian. Toby out: Ian out. That was how it worked for special advisers.

So Ian worried when he heard gossip that Toby was expendable. In the Commons tea room one day he heard a pompous but influential backbencher wonder out loud if Toby still had it in him. Ian felt uncomfortable when sensible compromises Toby had been happy to make with colleagues in other departments were written up in the press in ways that made Toby look weak – like risking pharma jobs in the UK by negotiating a price agreement that saved the NHS a few quid.

A major speech then might be an opportunity.

"So what's the speech about and where are you going to be giving it?" he asked Toby.

"It's a speech about competition policy – and where we are heading on that agenda. And we've just confirmed that I will give it in two weeks' time at the annual CBI President's dinner. Feels like the right audience for that sort of thing." He paused, and considered his next words, as he often did, looking around the room and then bringing his focus directly to Ian.

20

"So, Ian, I want you to help me get the content together, see if we can get a good announcement or two into it, and I want you to liaise with No.10 and Treasury."

Ian knew the form. This was often what he was asked to do when Toby felt a speech needed more energy and direction than the civil service were likely to give it.

"The main thing in the speech," Toby continued, "is to launch a consultation on toughening up fees for anti-competitive practices. It's good stuff and it should get a good reception – although some in the business lobby will resist it all."

Toby was a big man, square shouldered, thick faced, looking nothing like a Labour politician ought to look. He usually gave nothing away about his feelings, but something in the tone of his slightly north eastern accent made Ian realise he was excited about this speech.

"So what do you want out of it, Toby?" asked Ian. "I mean, what would be your ideal headline, and who would be cross and who would be happy with what you say?"

Toby hesitated; walked around his office. It was a fairly functional office enhanced by being on the corner with windows overlooking Westminster Abbey and Central Hall, Westminster, right in the heart of the power of government – Whitehall. The furniture was chunky and a bit "C-suite" – not Toby's choice but things he had inherited from the outgoing Secretary of State after his Party had won the elections. It was right not to spend taxpayer's money on re-kitting out the office, but very typically Toby. The avoidance of extravagance meant that the office did not feel like him at all. Ian felt it said that Toby was just a temporary occupant, ready to go at any moment.

"Well," Toby offered, "I think it's a pretty decent story. It should get a good write-up from the economics correspondents. Consumer press should like it and the consumer organisations. And, if we play it right, business might grin and bear it – 'could have been a lot tougher', that sort of thing."

Ian's shoulders slumped. He couldn't hide his frustration at Toby's lack of ambition. But he felt this was not the time to show it. Best to encourage Toby, get him excited, see if he could get himself a bit more room to play with.

"That's pretty good, Toby. So a speech that explains what we are doing, why we are doing it, makes the announcement and moves on."

"Yes, that sort of thing You know my style and approach. I really want people to understand that this isn't just a random policy move but fits our narrative of how we get Britain stronger, our firms more effective, so producing more wealth for the things we care about."

Heavy stuff. Important, really important.
But dull, dull, dull too.

Ian feared it wouldn't connect, wouldn't let the public get a glimpse of the passion and purpose of his boss.

"I'll get the private office to sort a few meetings with officials," Toby added, "and I'll have a word with the Chancellor of the Exchequer to tell him what we're doing as he has been quite involved with this policy. You let the grid people at Downing Street know what we are up to and make sure we have a decent slot in the timetable for our announcement."

Ian trotted back to his small office a few doors down from Toby's office. He got his PA to get the key official to come to his office as soon as she could manage it.

He sat quietly for a minute. It was a sort of false peace before what he knew was going to be quite a storm in preparing the speech. His mind was calm, contemplative, but ready to leap into action.

The lead official at the business department on competition policy was Sue Brown. Ian liked Sue. She was a bit can-do; lively, sharp and she seemed actually to believe in her brief. As a one-time civil servant himself, Ian knew this was a sort of fantasy. One year you were working on employment policy trying to make things fairer for those at work when their firm got taken over; the next you were doing almost the complete opposite in a job trying to reduce regulatory burdens on small firms. But for the two years or so you did the job, you sort of had to believe in it – at least a bit.

"Hi, Sue," Ian began, when she had arrived in his office. She straightened her skirt and carefully brushed her hair off her eyes before cautiously taking a seat. "The Secretary of State wants to announce a consultation on the new competition rules in a speech next Thursday. I just want to check exactly what is in that consultation document. I followed it a while back when we were discussing the outlines but I'm not sure exactly where we got to."

Sue smiled. As a mid-ranking official, your number didn't come up that often. Having the Secretary of State focus on your area suddenly put you in the spotlight. Some officials disliked that – they positively preferred keeping out of the way, in the shadows. In contrast, Ian could tell from the tone of her voice that Sue revelled in it.

"It is actually quite bold," she began eagerly. "It's changing the definition of anti-competitive practices so firms have less wriggle room. It's proposing the law be especially hard on them if they have some sort of monopoly or dominance in the market that gives them the power to behave in a bad way. And it quite sharply increases the penalties for being caught."

23

"Right," replied Ian. His mind was whirring. There was less in it than he had thought or hoped. And it was very technical.

"Can you give me an example of something we could catch businesses for if we had the new rules? I mean something that brings this to life."

"Well, I know what you mean," Sue responded with a nervous laugh. "Some of what it will allow us to catch and outlaw is invisible to most people. Like maybe a group of companies working together, acting as a cartel, to keep up cement prices. Or companies that are using the fact that they dominate the market to make the price of computer chips higher than they ought to be."

So, this could easily be a very "trade"-orientated speech. A decent write-up by the few journalists that followed this stuff and some applause from those economists and lawyers who focussed on all this. The question was: could it be more?

"What about the consumers, the punters, Sue? Anything for them?"

"Well of course," Sue answered with a hint of eagerness, unusual in a civil servant, "that's why we do all this. So, the result of all this is that prices should be cheaper for consumers. The cement thing is about the prices of houses and building work. The chips issue is about the price of computers."

This sounded more like it to Ian, as he reflected on what Sue had said after the meeting. It wasn't just that he wanted an easy headline – although he wanted that too – it was that he wanted to find a way of showing the average person what this was all about. Lose it in some complex language, dry as a bone, and you could never do that.

Early the next morning, with the sun shining bright through the big plate-glass windows of the Secretary of State's office, Ian met with Toby, with Sue and some other senior officials.

The meeting was to check that everyone within the Department was OK with the broad content of the speech. Toby seemed pretty happy that all was taking shape. He mainly saw the meeting as getting all the ducks in a row and briefing the departmental speech writer who was going to knock out the basic shape of the speech. But Ian, who knew the department in many ways better than his boss, sensed trouble.

Sue was asked to go through again what the changes might do. As he listened, Ian could feel that that she was soft-pedalling. No longer a major change in the regime to really get behind consumers, she presented it more as bits of tidying up to bring the law up to date.

It was when the Director of the so called "industry sponsorship" division spoke that it became clear what was going on. John Wright spoke slowly and precisely.

"I think, Secretary of State, that industry and their representative body, the CBI, will be able to – more or less – welcome the announcement." He paused, obviously aware that the next bit was not going to be music to the Secretary of State's ears.

"There will be of course some disquiet, though. Not only around the measures themselves but the appearance and implication it gives that they are up to something at present, behaving in a way that is detrimental to consumers."

Ian always hated the kind of leaden, emotion-free language that old hand civil servants used. Obsequious, yet evasive and dishonest at the same time. It always made him want to throw up or to scream. But the reason for him to say something at this point was more important than that. He needed to create room in Toby's mind for the place he wanted to take this speech to.

"But things *are* going on that are bad for consumers," he interjected. "That, surely, is why we are bringing the measure in."

The Director of Industry hesitated. He was an experienced Whitehall operator. He knew it was unwise to take on a special adviser too, obviously in front of his boss, not least as the Secretary of State would end up having to defend the adviser – his own personal appointment. Retreat a little now: fight on behind the scenes.

"Of course, that is the case Secretary of State, just as Ian says." He paused – clearly for effect – and then continued, "Although we must be careful not to imply that the whole of British industry is riddled with anti-competitive practices. After all, all the international organisations say our competition regime is pretty good."

"Interesting, John. Is that what you think, Sue?" asked Toby who, to Ian's relief, seemed to have sensed that Sue was under a bit of pressure. It was a tough position to put her in though – and there was tension in the room as they all waited to see how she would respond. How would she play off the fact that her superior, someone who would have a key role in writing her annual report and determining her promotion prospects, wanted this all to be played down, when she herself was really rather excited about its potential to shake up large swathes of British business?

"It is a pretty important step I think," said Sue, carefully picking her words. Having got that difficult first sentence out, Sue visibly grew in confidence. She now cleverly laced her pro consumer case with pro-business language.

"It is sort of the government saying that we don't think the best way to help you as businesses is to protect you from proper competition and scrutiny, but it is by making sure you have to play by the rules and operate in an open and fair market. That's what drives business forward, rewards the entrepreneur and the risk taker; the innovator. And we are going to do this – we are not going to pretend that there are no bad practices even if they are the exception."

"So good for consumers too?" Ian said, wanting some more positives for Toby now that Sue had got the business tone right.

"Yes, I think so," said Sue. "Where there have been anti-competitive practices going on that means prices have been higher." Looking at the Director of Industry she added, carefully, "Which must be true in some sectors even it by no means all of them."

Toby thanked Sue and John Wright for their thoughts and his more enthusiastic tone in his thanks to Sue gave no doubt where his sympathies lay.

Ian's relief must have been obvious to all as his face relaxed and he felt the tension flow out of him. He had at least got through this difficult moment with his plans intact.

The officials left and Ian had a chance to talk with Toby.

"Well that all seems pretty good," Toby began. "It looks like a strong announcement and now we just need a draft speech that brings it to life but doesn't rock the boat too much."

"Yes, I think it's going to be OK," said Ian knowing he was implicitly disagreeing with his boss and choosing his words and tone carefully. "I think, though, that we could really make it hum. These days, when prices always seem to be going up, this is an important moment to be on the side of ordinary families. Firms who push up prices beyond what they should be are in effect ripping people off, aren't they?"

"Yes, I suppose so," said Toby, with a quizzical tone as though he was aware that Ian was up to something, "but it's a pretty indirect effect. The main point of this change is to alter the ways firms go about trying to make money, so they spend a bit less time trying to avoid competition and a bit more trying to find what the consumer actually wants."

"That's fine, Toby," Ian said, "but I think this is much more than that. It's about our industrial strategy, yes. But it's also about being on the side of the ordinary person as they try to manage their weekly budget, and showing that we, as a government, get that."

There was a silence and Ian only gingerly stepped into it. "It's really good material if we do it right. And it would do no harm to have a loud voice from you out there at present."

Ian knew that Toby understood what he was getting at. Toby didn't really like the world he now found himself in, where you had to perform to the Prime Minister through the lens of the media and commentators if you didn't want to find yourself getting the chop. But Ian also knew that Toby was not totally naïve about the way things were.

"OK then," Toby said, conceding a bit of ground, "but let's not over-hype it and look ridiculous. And we must not become anti-business."

Ian had got what he wanted. He had some rope to play with. Now, how far could he take it?

He was confident he would be able to take Sue and the other officials with him and was pretty confident that John Wright would be a good civil servant and not kick up. The major obstacle now, as Ian saw it, was to keep those who were allergic to anything that sounded at all anti-business at bay – and that, at the moment, meant No.10. Ian pondered the options.

One way was to talk to the No.10 crew *now*, persuade them that this upping of the pro-consumer story was good for the government and for their boss, the PM, and then get the whole story formally slotted into the grid of announcements. All very "'by the book". But Ian resisted that approach. He knew the instinct at the moment of that venerable institution would be pretty cautious in doing anything that might annoy business – there had recently been a row on the position the government had taken on a bit of regulation to protect temporary workers and they wanted the temperature to reduce a bit. And in any case, if they thought it was a great announcement, they would want to steal it for themselves.

The alternative was to play it quietly, surprise them, or at least only open up fully nearer the time. Of course, that was not without risks for Toby. And there was a risk that Toby – or one of the officials – would let the cat out of the bag too early in any case. There were risks too for Ian. There were enough special advisers in No10 and Treasury who would know this was Ian's work and if he got away with it they would get their pound of flesh from him in the future.

But Ian felt it was worth the risk. He felt that Toby was in a weak position politically at present. A bit of good coverage, on the breakfast TV sofas, in the tabloid newspapers, was probably more powerful than keeping meekly in with the courtiers to those in power.

And in any case, he told himself, it is the right thing to do. Tackling the constant temptation of business to charge consumers more than they needed to was so, so right.

Taking all this forward now required a lot of work, but Ian tried to keep it quite tight with a fairly closed group working on it so as to reduce the risk of others wanting to put their oar in. Over the next few days, Ian worked closely with Sue on the policy side, with Jill, Toby's private office person who covered this area, with the "official" speech writer whose job was to churn out new drafts based on their conversations, and, less often, with Fred Argyle, the head of press. The speech started to take shape and some of the holes in it, policy wise, began to be filled.

But Ian knew it wasn't lifting off the page – not at all. It was too technocratic, too much about new roles and procedures. It needs, as Fred said, to force itself into the kitchens and front rooms of the public. It needed, as it emerged into public view, to be welcomed by charities and lobby groups for those on lower incomes, and by self-appointed consumer champions.

The speech needed to paint a picture; it needed to have enough in it so that a pre-briefed political editor could feel it worth giving it coverage because it appealed to their readers and because it clearly showed the direction the government was going.

Ian knew he wasn't a master at any of this. He was too much a policy specialist, so he did what he often did when he was a bit stuck and needed the input of a clear-thinking person not involved in the world of politics and policy, with its jargon and secret rules that he was part and parcel of. He talked to his wife.

They had been together for some years now. He knew that she thought that a lot of what he did was too much aimed at winning elections, and not enough at keeping to strong beliefs. Her eyes often rolled with despair when he tried to explain the latest policy shift. But she was usually ready to talk when he needed it.

He tried to explain the aim of the policy change to her as they chatted over a late supper. They were sat across from each other at a rough wooden table that had seemed a good idea at the time but was too uneven to work well when they had guests. His wife looked tired, her eyes clouded and unfocussed and her hair straggling down more than usual. It wasn't really the time to engage her in this, but he went for it anyway.

"What this change to the rules does is make it harder for firms to charge customers more than they should."

"And why does that matter to anyone?" asked his wife, already sounding bored of the whole thing.

But Ian realised that she had homed in straight on to the thing that Ian had taken as a given.

He managed to check himself from saying something annoying and condescending like, "Well nobody wants to pay more than they have to." That wasn't the issue.

"It's because if prices are lower it makes their pay packet go further – their own work now buys more."

"Well, that sounds like something worth having," she replied, taking a sip from the large glass of red wine she was clutching. "Anything else?"

"Well, I guess," continued Ian, feeling animated now that he had freed himself from the policy way of thinking, "it means those guys don't get rich on the back of over-charging ordinary people, people who can't afford it."

"OK," said his wife, leaning forward across the table. She had always been a bit more radical than him and it showed now. "You need a phrase, a picture, to get across that people who work hard all day are angry that they have to pay more than they need just so some big boss fat cat can line their pockets. It's sort of like theft."

Ian hugged her hard. What a wife! Now he knew what territory he needed this speech to be in.

He slept on it and the next day, after playing around with different phrases, came up with something along the lines of "the hard working not wanting their purse to be lighter just so someone else can make more profits". That would do for the moment. And he went to talk about it to Toby.

Toby looked a bit distracted when Ian got in to see him and was wandering around the room with a cup of tea in his hand. He'd just been in a meeting with a delegation of around ten Chinese business guys and wanted to tell Ian about it. It was important stuff. Ian felt proud to work for

Toby and pleased the government had such a good and conscientious minister in such a key role. But Ian was getting impatient so while he listened he was also waiting for his moment. Yes, it was interesting to know how smart the Chinese were and what they thought of the prospects for investment in the UK, but he wanted to get Toby's focus.

When Toby had come to a natural halt, Ian was able to get him absorbed into the world of the speech and to describe what he was trying to do make the speech have more bite.

Toby listened and after a few seconds, listened hard. He leaned back in his chair with his hands clasped and kept his focus on Ian as he spoke. Ian loved it when Tony was in this mood; it showed he was starting to get into the essence of the speech.

"You know," he began, "I see so many of my constituents who work pretty hard, not to achieve some spectacular standard of living but just to have a decent life. And it's hard," – he emphasised and repeated that word "hard" – "hard to find and keep the job, often not well paid. Hard to find the rent or afford the mortgage on a place that will just about 'do'. Hard to afford the basics you need today: the washing machine, the car, the computer. Maybe, maybe have a decent holiday once in a while." He got up from his chair, but he kept talking. "And that idea, that someone is charging you more than they need to, really is like they are being robbed. It really is."

"Robbed," repeated Ian, "that's right, Toby. But it's quite a strong word. And it is not about GBH; it's like something you almost don't notice."

"Yes, you're right," agreed Toby, "but it needs some force, some sense of anger." Toby, the often quiet and consensus man had had his heart touched by all this. Ian now had to deliver.

Ian continued to think and also to work with the team on the rest of the speech. Most of it was fairly standard fare – the economic policy of the government; the need for innovation and enterprise; the support government was giving firms in various ways. But it was a bit sharper and more direct than usual in some parts, as they tried to build up to the tougher competition policy story and integrate the consumer into the story. Here the speech talked about not mollycoddling industry and the mistake of over-protecting it from international or domestic competition. It was a delicate balance.

While the speech was still not quite there, Ian felt this was going to be an important and insightful speech in terms of the positioning of the government. That meant he now really ought to keep his masters and betters at Downing Street in the loop. He'd kept them out of it this far – now he needed to bring them in.

The easiest thing for Ian to do was to talk to his opposite number in the Downing Street Policy Unit, to tell her the basic story of the planned speech. He knew that Sheila, who covered this area, would like its general flavour. Sure, others in and around the PM would be nervous, not wanting to do anything that might annoy the fabled and media-friendly captains of industry with so many other sensitive issues around; but he would leave her to manage the No10 internals at this point. She was one of the grown-ups in No.10 – not a panicky type, not someone so impressed with their own power that they liked to lord it over everyone else, especially departmental special advisers.

But even so, he didn't tell her everything, just the broad themes they were trying to get across. And he felt a bit bad about that because he knew that he was out to stir things up a bit, that he was to some extent blind-siding Sheila, and that if he succeeded, she would suffer a bit of backlash from her No.10 colleagues.

"OK," said Sheila, when he had gone through it with her. "Just don't go too far, Ian; we have a lot of stuff going on with the CBI at the moment and after all the arguments on temporary workers we don't want to annoy them where we really don't need to. And make sure I see a final copy of the speech in good time."

"Of course," answered Ian, an answer that seemed to give her reassurance without saying anything frankly dishonest. He could now go back to focussing on getting the speech right.

"Robbed" still felt too strong to Ian. It conjured up someone with a stocking over their head, a bag of swag and probably a bit of violence. He couldn't use it. It needed to be softer – but similar.

He left the idea swirling, hoping the right word would come to him at some point.

The speech was now only a few days away. It was perfectly adequate, and he was reasonably happy with it – and so was Toby. But Ian still felt it was falling short, giving up an opportunity both to tell a story he believed in and also to get people to sit up and notice.

But Ian knew he was aiming for more than this. He knew that if he could get the words right and get it out to the media in the right way, he might tilt the whole tone of the government towards one that was more strongly pro-consumer, and a bit anti-big business. He knew it and he wanted it.

Inspiration came from an unexpected place.

As he walked back home from the Tube that evening, he popped into the supermarket to buy some bread and cheese that his wife had asked him to get. He walked down the vegetable aisle and noticed a guy in front of him with his wallet sticking out of his back pocket, just waiting and asking for it to be stolen. That was it; he had the phrase.

And now the next morning, he quickly worked it into the speech and talked the whole thing through with his boss.

Toby liked the speech and he liked the phrase Ian had come up with, but now he went through a nervous phase. He knew this was more than a standard competition policy speech and he both wanted that and feared it. He made little comments to Ian that signalled this discomfort. "Do you think that bit needs amending to go down better with the car industry? Why have you written it so harshly there?"

To try and counter this, Ian got him to read out the speech a couple of times so that he began to enjoy saying it, feeling comfortable with it, so that he took ownership of it, especially its key passages. It had to be his speech, not Ian's and now having gone through this process, it had indeed become Toby's. That key transition – from speech-writer to speech-giver ownership – was done.

Now it was right for Ian to start to tell some of the rest of the team the key bits of the speech, some of which was new to them.

"This is the line we're going to brief for tomorrow morning. What do you think?" Fred, the press man was keen. But Sue was the key person he wanted to hear from. She read the passage and Ian waited. He knew some would not like what he had done, but that was their tough luck. But he really valued Sue's view.

"It's strong, Ian, and it will ruffle a fair number of feathers. But I like it." She hesitated, clearly with a bit more to say. "Not sure John Wright will though," she added softly.

"Don't worry, Sue. The Secretary of State has signed it off, so we have clearance. I'll deal with John."

Ian played around with just not telling John Wright until the deed was done. But that felt a subterfuge too far. Ian may not really have liked Wright, but he was a decent guy, doing his job. And he was Director of the industry sponsorship team at the Business department. He would have to take some of the flak from business when they heard it. He deserved to know. Ian got his office to get John round to see him.

"Thanks for all your help, John," said Ian. "The Secretary of State is very pleased with the way the speech has come out. He thinks that, thanks to your work, as well as Sue's, we have got the balance about right."

Wright shuffled, clearly suspicious. "Can I see the final version," he asked, "so I can brief some of the key players and stop them being surprised?"

Ian looked Wright in the eye and held it for more than the usual amount. He was not the Secretary of State, just an unelected special adviser. He needed to protect his boss but not to overplay his hand. There was a risk; but decency demanded he take it.

"Here is a copy of the speech, John. Most of it you've seen before. We've just played around with some of the phrases, some of the rhetoric."

But he needed to say more.

"The Secretary of State is happy for you to brief the CBI and a few others in general terms; but we want to hold the full speech back for the moment so don't circulate it or quote from it yet please."

As Wright left the office Ian didn't know how he would react when he read it. Would he try to make a fuss and get to the Secretary of State? Or would he roll with the punch?

Ian knew this was tough for Wright as he had been a civil servant himself in the past. Whatever Wright's personal feelings, he would feel a duty to tell the Secretary of State that a key group would be unhappy. But, more than this, his relationship with the key players he had to work with would become frayed. They would realise that he did not have the clout he claimed to have or at least inferred he had, and they would work that less closely with him in the future. He would lose face – he would be diminished.

Of course, he might ignore the steers that Ian had given and tip off the CBI or even try to go round the back of Ian to No.10 and get Toby to back off that way. If he was clever, he'd get the CBI to tell No.10. But it was risky. He'd risk his standing with Toby – a danger while he remained Secretary of State.

It was time to talk to Toby again. The speech was due the next day, and Ian needed to get the press office to brief key media people soon if they were to make the morning editions. Ian didn't want to take the last step without Toby being 100 per cent aware. He met Toby alongside the head of press, Fred Argyle.

"So the speech is all done, and you're happy with it. The only thing to sort is the press and the stakeholder handling. Fred's helping me with the press side."

"Yes, Ian, but can I just check with you guys that No.10 are happy."

Ian hesitated, coughed, and played for time as he thought of the right response. He could feel a small bead of sweat forming on his forehead as he knew he was going to have to answer this in a very partial way.

"They know in general what it says but we've not sent the full speech over yet…" That was half the truth and after a pause Ian gave a bit more. Although they have asked."

"Ian," said Toby, looking angry and quite menacing with it in the way only a big man can, "you've got to let them have it. Now. I don't want to cause any trouble with them." Ian felt this was much more for Fred's ears than his own; of course Toby knew they could not let No.10 know exactly what they were going to say too early or they would demand a tone down.

"We will," said Ian, "but can you give me the go-ahead

for us to brief the speech as if we don't go in the next few hours. we will miss the deadlines."

"OK," said Toby, "but do it with care."

Ian knew it had been left ambiguous as to whether he was supposed to brief *only* if No.10 had cleared the speech or could go ahead now. He also knew Tony well enough to know that he had deliberately left that ambiguity. He was leaving it to Ian to decide in a way that gave Toby deniability should he need it. Thanks, Toby, thought Ian ruefully. Thanks a million.

The newspapers the next day loved the story.

Stop "pick-pocketing" us at the cash tills: Toby the consumers' friend slams the supermarkets, screamed a tabloid.

Government accuses big business of "pick-pocketing" hard working consumers with anti-competitive practices said the more detached tone of the FT on its front page.

The Guardian was a bit fruitier: *Government declares war on big retailers – the real "pick pockets".*

Ian knew they had done well. That they had broken through. But he knew there was going to be a price to pay.

The phone calls from No.10 started almost as soon as the first editions were out. They went to Ian at home, to his mobile, to the private office, all over the place. The gist of them was pretty clear: "What the fuck do you think you are doing and why didn't we know?"

Ian had sent Sheila the speech but at a time when he knew she would have left the office. He had also texted her to alert her to that fact, but admittedly he had only done that later that evening after they had briefed the press and when she would most likely be in bed.

They developed a line to use with Downing Street fast. "We briefed you a while back on the basic story – the

38

strengthening of competition policy to help consumers. We only finished the text late. We sent it to you. The press picked up on one line to play it up. We will do media to explain it."

No.10 would know it was no accident; all the press had picked up on the same bit of the speech. A bit too obvious – indeed you would have to be a lousy journalist not to.

But it was credible and would work unless someone really got to the PM. After all, sensible political press and strategy folk in No.10 would know it was a great story. And a bit of CBI and big business unhappiness could be lived with when all was said and done.

Ian was pretty tired. He'd had to push hard to get that speech in good shape, hard to get Toby in the right place, hard to make it a speech that people might remember. He had had to step on a few toes, tell a few half-truths, and embarrass a few good people. But that was his job and today it had gone well. On his way home he bought some flowers for his wife, and he sent a thank you text to Sheila at No.10.

And tomorrow, it would start all over again.

Not All Ministers Are the Same

One day Alice got an unexpected call from Jane, the private secretary to Nigel Smith, a fairly new junior minister at the department. Jane was the rather shy civil servant who looked after his office.

"Can you spare the time for a cup of coffee, Alice?"

It was an unusual request.

Private secretaries to junior ministers rarely called the Secretary of States' special advisers. Jane's job was to help her minister get through his papers in a sensible order, help him prioritise his day and feed his decisions back into the civil service machine. Normally Alice would not get very involved.

But Jane got a bit stranger still. "Could we meet at the café on the corner of Marsham Street and Great Peter Street?"

If the idea of a coffee was a surprise to Alice, Jane wanting to meet in one of the cafés a bit away from the office threw her off balance. Alice didn't consider herself a suspicious person, but she beat her fingers on the desk trying to fathom what this might all be about.

Alice kept in touch with all the private secretaries to the junior ministers. She felt it was part of her job in supporting the Secretary of State, a way of knowing how the team were all getting on – and keeping an eye on them of course. But she didn't really know Jane very well. In fact, she was wracking her brain to recall ever really having had a chat with Jane about anything of importance before.

She didn't really know much about Nigel either. He'd been parachuted into the department in a "mini" re-shuffle of government posts a few months ago. His predecessor as Minister for Employment Relations in the Business Department had been a pretty straightforward woman.

Crucially, Alice had known she was loyal to the Secretary of State and would not be playing any political or personal games that meant she needed a lot of watching.

But the new, incoming minister was another thing altogether.

He seemed to have climbed above his colleagues pretty fast to arrive at a ministerial post far quicker than was normal. And that, so the House of Commons tea-room gossip went, was less due to his talent and more because of his closeness to the powerful Chancellor of Exchequer, the boss of the Treasury.

Rumour was that they were old mates from university. But whatever the reason, Nigel Smith was known to be one of the Chancellor's inner circle.

Alice strode purposefully towards the café – late as usual. She was aware that her shirt was a bit creased and she was annoyed with herself for always letting that happen. But she went slower as she got nearer, wary of whatever this was going to be about.

Jane was in the café already, nursing a cappuccino at a small table in the noisy, and slightly rushed atmosphere. She flipped her hair back behind her glasses. Alice queued up for her own coffee and then joined her. They made a bit of small talk – holidays, a bit of work gossip and questions about Jane's children that Alice had luckily remembered existed – and then Alice moved the conversation on.

"So, what's up, Jane? How can I help?"

Jane smiled and talked rather softly so that Alice had to lean in to hear her above the café hubbub.

"Well, this is totally private, Alice, and it may be nothing," she began with a nervous, whispered laugh, "but I'm not quite sure what Nigel is up to on the employment relations brief."

"Go on," said Alice, feeling goosebumps of tension on her arms. "What do you mean?" She tried hard not to look too alarmed. Was Nigel trying to undermine what her boss was pushing for? Why would he do that?

"So, as far as I know," Jane said, "the Secretary of State wants us to push hard for as strong employment rights as possible for women returning to work."

"Yes, she does," Alice said.

"Well, I'm not sure that is what Nigel is pushing for, at least not in all aspects." She looked nervously at Alice, also half checking those going in and out of the café as if fearful of being spotted chatting with a special adviser.

Alice squeezed her coffee tight and tried to keep calm. *What is Jane trying to tell me?* She didn't want Jane getting into trouble; but she desperately needed to know more.

"What exactly do you mean, Jane? Which bits are disturbing you?"

"Well, none really," she answered to Alice's frustration. "I'm not spying on Nigel, and he is a clever man and may know what he is doing." It wasn't clear if she was ever going to get to the point, but it was as if she could read Alice's mood and so more at last gushed out.

"I don't think he is really pushing very hard with our officials and with other departments for the right to work part time to be extended beyond those with young children."

So that was it. Nigel was trying to undermine a key policy of Alice's boss.

The Secretary of State was keen that anyone with caring responsibilities should be able to request the right to work part time. She had made that very clear in a major speech shortly after they had been elected. True, it mattered most for those with young kids and that was why the government had brought that right into law in its early days. But the need to care doesn't go away when your children are older

42

or if you are looking after your elderly parents. So that right needed to be extended.

That was the Secretary of State's position and everyone in the Department knew it. And it was incumbent upon junior ministers to represent that position in conversations and debates with other Departments and internally with civil servants.

But why would Nigel be against that?

She picked at her fingernails, her mind buzzing.

But then it all clicked. She knew business really did not like the idea of extending the right – just another burden on poor old businesses, trying to get on with making a crust.

The obvious thing for the CBI, the voice of business, to do in this situation? Go to the Chancellor, tell him your worries, tell him that if it goes ahead there will be a backlash from business. And that road, thought Alice with some alarm, led straight to Nigel not supporting this agenda.

Alice realised that Jane could read some of this in her face and that it was slightly panicking her.

"I'm not certain of that, Alice," Jane began, adjusting her glasses as she spoke. "I mean I may be being unfair to him, and he may just be playing it in a subtle way. But…" She looked at Alice in a needy way that got under Alice's skin, "… I just wanted to let you know."

Later, back at the office, Alice wrestled with this issue. She could tell her boss, but it was only passing on a bit of gossip and speculation. It might in any case be nonsense: Jane didn't seem to the best judge of people. And she had to be careful in getting her boss into a confrontation with Nigel and hence with the Chancellor – possibly all for nothing.

On the Tube home to her flat pretty late that night, Alice tried to work out what to do. Maybe best just to leave it be. So what if a junior minister is trying to undermine the

Secretary of State on an issue? It's happened before, it will happen again; it is the Secretary of State's word that matters anyway; you don't want a fight with the Chancellor, and this is hardly the key issue of the day. *So relax, Alice.*

She noticed a mum with a toddler in a pushchair, no doubt picked up from a childminder after a late shift at work. She had the right to request part-time work now, but what about all the other mums, daughters – and dads – packed in here. She couldn't just ignore the situation with Nigel.

In the morning Alice asked if Jane could find her a time in the next few days to meet with Nigel – "just to catch up" she said, since they had not really managed to do that so far. It sounded a pretty thin reason to Alice and she felt her heart beat a bit faster at the thought that Nigel might think it strange too. But some sort of conversation with him was the best way ahead that she could think of. In fact, Jane found them a slot that afternoon. It appeared Nigel was keen to chat.

Alice knew the way to his office. You went out of her little office, down the corridor along the 4th floor, past several meeting rooms following the boundaries of the full height atrium in this late 1990s, too-much-glass building. Then past the Secretary of State's office on the left; a right-hand turn and the second door on the left. That was the door that led to the Private Office, the way you were supposed, as an official, to enter a minister's office, not via the first, "direct" door, which was just for external guests.

Jane smiled nervously as Alice put her head round the door. She showed her into the minister's office and then retreated rather abruptly to leave the field to Alice. Alice almost leapt back in surprise as she peered into the room.

She had been there a couple of times before with the previous minister: basic furniture with a desk to the left and a sofa and two chairs in the more "informal" space to the side of the desk. But clearly things had changed drastically with Nigel's arrival. The desk was now in the middle of the room, the sofa was gone. Two modern steel and leather chairs faced each other with a third in front of the desk. But what Alice noticed even more was the lighting; no longer an old-fashioned strip light but an uplighter to one side and a spotlight lamp on the desk. With it starting to get dark outside, the effect was striking.

It was rather nice; quite classy, quite relaxed. But it didn't feel like an office for getting business done.

Nigel was charm itself, greeting her with a big smile.

He offered Alice a chair and before Jane left the room she asked if Alice and Nigel wanted a drink. Alice asked for a normal cup of tea and she tried not to show surprise when Nigel asked for a ginger and lemon tea. And if that wasn't a bit unusual in Whitehall land, the next thing she knew was that Nigel had flicked on some music via his computer; some calm, gentle, classical music at a low pitch and volume. It was definitely not the ordinary set up in her experience of ministers. But it was rather pleasant and she couldn't help smiling.

"It's good to know you are part of the team here, Alice," Nigel said in a warm, friendly, yet a bit creepy, way. His smile was welcoming yet a bit knowing, suggesting they were part of a little cabal.

"Charlie says you are one of the best and I should make sure we work together."

Charlie was the Chancellor of the Exchequer, except that very few called him "Charlie". Most referred to him as "the Chancellor" and even the closest of his Cabinet colleagues spoke of him as "Charles".

"Thanks," said Alice, feeling the heat in her cheeks with the flattery but also wondering what was going on.

"I hope," said Nigel, "that I can be useful to the Secretary of State who has a really big and important task in this department." And then, looking Alice firmly in the eye, he added, "And that we can see how to get a bit more support from the Treasury over a few things."

Alice sipped at her tea. Nigel was charming. But she didn't like the feel of it. He was being too nice. Was Nigel really a useful new member of the team with good links to the Chancellor? Or was he a spy in the camp, keeping "Charlie" posted on what the Business department and her boss were up to?

Maybe Nigel felt a bit of Alice's discomfort. "I don't want to undermine anything," he said. Not half thought Alice, feeling even more uncomfortable. "But I can help you and the Secretary of State by sounding out the lie of the land over at the Treasury and what Charlie's team at No 11 are up to."

Alice tried to probe a little on the issue of the moment, asking Nigel how he thought it was going on the right to request. He said all the right things in reply. She wouldn't get very far in that way.

But Nigel was right about the usefulness of his access and insider knowledge of the key Treasury players. He was as good as his word in the next few days in the run up to the annual Budget, helping the department rather unexpectedly secure a slug of capital money for some facilities to help set up "advanced manufacturing" pilots.

And he worked with Alice to get the Treasury to lean on some of the bigger companies so that they did not publicly oppose a tightening up of the competition rules, rules that firms never really liked despite their supposed allegiance to open and fair competition.

So on the surface Nigel was proving the perfect junior minister: he got on with the job without needing guidance all the time, but had good enough judgement to come and ask if he wasn't sure exactly which way the boss might want to play things. Alice no longer went all tense at the mention of his name.

But she still didn't quite trust Nigel – and was haunted by what Jane had told her.

She couldn't just let this drop. She had to find out what Nigel was up to. Asking him was not going to work – he was too smart for that. She needed another way.

Alice decided to set a trap: an attempt to flush this out one way or another.

The next day, after a night of a disturbed sleep as her mind whirred, she met with the official who led the work in the right-to-request area. She asked him about the analysis the department had done on the costs to business of changes to the extension of the right-to-request part-time work. She also asked for a summary of the representations the department had received from those opposed to that move. To her dismay it turned out there were quite a lot of them, some citing different types of evidence to support their case. She felt anger well up in her even though it wasn't really a surprise. What did businesses care about the way normal families tried to live their lives?

But this might also give her the ammunition she needed to test Nigel out.

"Has the minister been given all these hostile answers to the consultation?"

"Not yet, we are just putting all the information and analysis into shape ready to put in a submission to ministers in a few days' time."

Alice took a risk. "I'd like the Minister of State – Nigel – to have a look at this to see what he thinks before we get to wider discussion with the Secretary of State and the rest of Whitehall."

"That's no problem," answered the official, grateful to have their work taken seriously and likely to get an airing. "I should say that there is a lot of material also showing it will benefit the economy, be good for women and equality – we have lots of submissions and analysis saying that too."

Alice smiled as she felt for the official trying to be as balanced as possible. "So what would you like me to do?" asked the official.

"Just put a short submission up to Nigel," said Alice, "telling him that this is some early work from those against the proposals and you want a sense check as to whether he thinks this sort of material is helpful and how to present it."

That seemed fine. The deed was done, the plot was activated. And because she asked specifically to be copied into the submission she knew when Nigel had received it. The question now was what would Nigel do with the information he was now party to, information potentially damaging to the Secretary of State's viewpoint, information that could be used to try and pull the plug on her aim of extending the right? If he kept it to himself, he was probably on side. If it turned up in Treasury attacks, she would know what was going on.

The key test came at the next Cabinet sub-committee meeting to consider employment issues. This was a meeting that Alice's boss herself not only attended but chaired, and although the Chancellor himself was not present, the Chief Secretary to the Treasury, his number two with his own seat in Cabinet, was. And on the agenda was an update of progress towards extending the right to request part-time work.

This meeting took place in one of the meeting rooms in the House of Commons, rather than in the Cabinet Office – not an unusual occurrence when ministers needed to be near the Chamber as a vote in Parliament was expected towards the end of the scheduled meeting time. It was a long room, below ground level. No windows, but some big, dark brown bookcases with old, venerable volumes of Hansard, the record of Parliamentary debates. Unlike some rooms Alice had been in, it had no glorious wood panelling or old fireplaces, or grand old pictures of old parliamentarians. It was pretty bare, slightly off white, and a little too cold. It was not a room you wanted to stay too long in.

Special advisers were not generally welcome at these events. Cabinet Office, who policed the committees, did not like it – special advisers did not really fit into their view of how the constitution should work. So usually Alice didn't try to go. But this time she'd told her boss she wanted to hear how things were going and her boss told her just to come and sit with her principal private secretary. It was easier when your boss was chairing the Committee – nobody was going to openly object.

Of course, Nigel was there too. They had briefly mentioned the meeting in the round up at the weekly ministerial team meeting on the Monday morning in the Secretary of State's office.

"I'm at the sub-committee on employment rights on Wednesday," Nigel had volunteered as they had gone round the table. "You are chairing it. Quite a lot of things on the agenda – where we are on the minimum wage is the top issue."

"Anything else?" Alice asked with a slight urgency in her voice, wanting to prompt a bit more out of Nigel. Would he volunteer the other issue?

"Yes, a few other things. Some proposals on information and consultation with workers in larger firms." Alice could feel herself tensing up – was he going to leave out the issue she was trying to test him on?

"And," continued Nigel, "a discussion of what we

should propose on extending rights to request part-time work. That one looks like it's getting quite heated as various departments are objecting as they are being lobbied by the sectors they work with who say it will be too big a change for them to handle."

The Secretary of State suddenly sprang to attention. She tended to see these collective team meetings as formalities, to be put up with to show she cared about her team, rather than genuine interactive sessions discussing policy, or tactics. She dealt with those more tricky issues in one-to-one meetings.

"Well, Nigel, you know where we stand, so let me know if there is anything I need to do to keep the agenda going our way."

"Oh don't worry," laughed Nigel, "I know very well where you stand, and I'll argue the case strongly and we will win."

As she sat down at the sub-committee meeting, Alice felt the beginnings of a headache, and she noticed her hands shaking ever so slightly as she searched in her bag for some medication. As a fairly experienced political operator that surprised even herself. It wasn't nerves about the outcome of the meeting. She knew enough departments were on side that they would get something close to what her boss wanted, even with some compromises. It was about how things would play out with Nigel.

She was pretty sure that Nigel himself would stick to the departmental line on the part-time issue. Actually, he went further, arguing enthusiastically for the case on economic grounds as well as on the equity and the morality of such a move.

But there was more to the test than that. What would the Treasury say? Had Nigel tipped them off with the information he had access to? Would their contribution show this or not?

As they went around the table, with each departmental minister giving their comments from their own department's perspective, Alice felt her stomach churn. How would she know if Nigel had fed the information that she had made sure had got to him, and that could be of help to the Business department's enemies, to the Treasury? What would be the giveaway? Could she assume that if they used a fact that had been given to Nigel by the department, that that was where they had got it from? And if they didn't say anything, was Nigel in the clear – or were they just keeping their powder dry for another day, one more important than this sub-committee?

The Treasury spoke last. The Chief Secretary started off in classic Treasury fashion. While the Treasury understood fully that this was an important measure, he said that of course there had to be a degree of caution about its impact on the economy.

Alice wrinkled her face tight. She was annoyed with this "we must be careful" approach. She felt that he was more or less just reading out the brief prepared for him by his officials, not thinking about what was right for the nation – or even the Party. She knew that the job of the Chief Sec was to keep an eye on just about every item of government activity that might cost money or affect the ability of the economy to grow. That job could be so overwhelming that he would no doubt rarely have time to prep for a meeting but would have to rely on his civil service brief. But even so.

But as the Chief Sec came to the end of his contribution, asking for some phasing or even exemptions for smaller firms, Alice realised that there had been virtually no numbers, no case studies in what the Chief Sec had said – despite the material that Nigel would have had available to him.

What a relief. It was going well. Alice was feeling OK. Nigel was clean.

But then, to her horror, the chair, her Secretary of State, unexpectedly interjected. It was obvious to Alice, from the way she was carrying herself, her head to one side, that she wanted to make a big point. But would this end up with another test for Nigel, one he might not pass?

"Thanks to the Chief Secretary and to all departments who have spoken. I know some of you said you are a little uncertain of the impacts of this change. We will take that on board as best we can in developing the policy. Of course there will be some uncertainty but we all know this is the right policy. But I don't want us to discuss this again if there isn't a real, well-documented issue, not just a few scare stories and lobbying tales. So, let's hear any hard evidence you have now, in this room."

It was a bold move from her boss, aimed at disarming the doubters and wreckers in one blow; challenging them to put up or shut up. Or even to argue that this was an unreasonable request.

It was also a key moment for Alice. It dared the Treasury to use any material on costs and case studies that it had – and maybe that would include the treasure chest that had been given to Nigel.

There was an atmosphere of expectation as the room went silent. The Chair looked sharply at each person around the table in turn. She had raised the bar high and there was silence. She looked hard at the Chief Secretary. "Anything from the Treasury?" she asked.

"No, Chair," replied the Chief Secretary, "nothing that strong. We would want to err on the safe side and phase the right in. But you know that already."

The tension in the room immediately eased and for a brief second all the energy rushed out of Alice. She felt her shoulders relax, her breathing calm down. The end of the meeting happened with her hardly noticing.

So, Nigel had passed the test and he could have Alice's trust – at least for the moment.

Alice felt her heart beat slow down. Not only had her boss got what she wanted from the meeting, but Nigel looked to be in the clear. He had his chance to feed damaging information to the Treasury and it looked like he hadn't taken it.

It was a relief. She had come to rather like Nigel with his rather strange habits and peculiar teas. And he could be a good ally. She caught his eye and he smiled.

She felt good about that. Her judgement had been right all along. Not everyone was playing the game. There were good people.

But then she wondered. Did his smile mean he'd seen her plan and dodged the bullet? Who knew?

As she walked out of the meeting with her Secretary of State, she noted that Nigel did not join them but stayed back to talk to the Chief Secretary.

What did that mean? Alice didn't know.

In politics, you never knew.

The Source

"Can you go to the Permanent Secretary's office please?" Will looked up from the screen on his untidy desk and scratched his curly mop of hair. He didn't quite register what he was being asked.

"The Permanent Secretary says, can you come now." It was now more of an instruction than a request.

"OK, OK, let me just save this document," he replied, fiddling about with the mouse and suddenly finding it difficult to work out which button to press.

"What's it about then?" he asked the junior civil servant who he recognised as being one of the team that worked for the Permanent Secretary, the most senior official in the Department and the sort of CEO.

"I don't know I'm afraid," she answered with a sort of friendly smile that seemed a bit odd in the circumstances. "Must be quite important if she wants to see you straight away."

Will straightened his tie, took his suit jacket off the back of the chair and put it on carefully. He ran a hand through his hair – to no real effect.

This meeting could be about anything, but it sounded a bit ominous. It was the first time he had been called so urgently to go and see the Permanent Secretary in his year as one of the two special advisers in the department. His boss was the politician, the Secretary of State, who he spoke to a lot; but the Permanent Secretary mattered. He got on fine with her but apart from an introductory talk and a couple of times when she had wanted to check with him that the Secretary of State was happy with the service he was getting, they had always met in meetings with other people present.

Had his boss been caught doing something wrong and

was he about to be told about it? Had a junior minister caused trouble with their staff and was he about to be asked to help sort it out? Will shook his head. It could be anything.

He went through the Permanent Secretary's outer office and was shown straight through to her main office, a rather drab modern room with some vaguely interesting modern art hung on white walls between the big picture windows overlooking Westminster Abbey. It was quite a view and Will would have liked to have stared out of the window for a bit. Sharon Ings welcomed him and ushered him gently to the chair in front of her desk – carefully avoiding the other option of the sofa and armchairs to the side of the room. That felt serious.

"Thanks for coming over, Will," Sharon said, looking at him hard and seriously.

Will kept silent, nervous to hear what this was all about, but also intrigued.

Sharon began. "We have been told that tomorrow in the newspaper there is going to be a piece saying that sources close to the Secretary of State are deeply unhappy with the Energy Regulator. The Secretary of State, they will say, thinks, and I quote, that 'the Regulator is not on board, a bit off beam, too fixed on approaches that were being pursued by the previous government'."

It's pretty serious, as you will understand. Independence of the regulators to make decisions without political interference has been the cornerstone of our regulation for some time, and the government committed itself to maintaining in its Manifesto."

Ings paused, looking directly at Will.

Will made no comment. He tried to look blank.

"Do you know anything about this, Will?"

He said nothing. And he tried not to play with his hands.

"Do you know how the journalist might have got this story?"

It was the moment of truth. Will's mind was in full throttle and he could feel the sweat begin to moisten his hands.

If he said yes, then what would happen to him? Where would her probe go next? If they thought he had done wrong, would he just be reprimanded, told off, or would it be much worse? Would he lose his job? Never able to find another one? An outcast with his political friends? Would his boss be caught in the mess and be brought down? Would the government suffer?

If he said no, would there be a full investigation, and how would it proceed? Would it try to prove it was him, or would it look for others? What would the journalist say if they were asked?

After all, as Will knew, those thoughts that the Permanent Secretary had read out, were shared not only by him and his boss, but by most of the civil service. He knew that because they had discussed it pretty recently in a meeting the Secretary of State had had with senior officials.

In any case, was it such a bad a thing if this material appeared in the press? Many would agree with that critique of the Regulator – certainly the Party's supporters, who thought he was a snooty and aloof man, full of economic theory and unaware of the lives of ordinary families. Set that against some theoretical, highfalutin' idea that the regulators had to be completely independent and what was the trade-off? Especially as this regulator had been appointed by the other political party shortly before what they knew would be an election defeat.

"No," Will answered. "I don't know how the journalist got this story."

Ings didn't give up that easily.

"You do know this journalist don't you, Will?"

"I know most of the journalists that cover our patch – the specialist ones, not the political lobby. It's part of my job. So yes, I know this one." It was a decent enough line, but he knew the next question would be coming.

"And have you spoken to this journalist recently?"

Will glanced around the room and then came back to look the Permanent Secretary in the eyes. As it happened, he had not spoken to this journalist for a couple of weeks. So it was an easy answer. "No, not recently."

Sharon seemed to visibly relax.

"Thanks, Will. This is going to be a nasty bit of press and I think you know I needed to ask you these questions."

"Of course," said Will, hoping he sounded calm and relaxed.

In fact he was seething.

The minute something happened, the old-style civil servants like Sharon went for the special advisers. No worry that her senior officials leaked like a sieve, something Will had learned over time. How come the journalists so often knew about stuff going on in the department before even he or the Secretary of State did? Well at least one journalist had hinted to him that if you knew where they drank after work you could always pick up gossip, and that some senior officials were always partial to a bit of spin themselves over a decent lunch.

But the easy prey for the senior civil service to accuse were the special advisers – the people they really did not like anyway.

Will returned to his office, sat back in his chair with his hands behind his head and thought deeply. He had indeed spoken with the journalist, but it was weeks ago, and he was certain he had not used those sort of words. He would have signalled that there were some doubts about the Regulator

– but it would have been general, not mentioning his boss. Maybe he had said a bit too much, and that made him feel tense and worried. But no, he really had not said much at all.

Yes, he knew the Secretary of State thought all this but so did a lot of officials. Even the Prime Minister's special advisers were sceptical as Will knew from meetings with No.10 after the Regulator had said something publicly that was clearly – and seemingly deliberately – unhelpful to the government in the way it was worded.

So it was not at all clear that he was the actual source. True, he may have given the journalist enough of a sniff of a story to go and get some more quotes on it from others but that was a whole different issue. In his mind he was clear: he had done nothing wrong. He was not the source. He ruffled his hair, breathed more slowly and tried to get on with the rest of his day.

Things went quiet, although it all stayed in Will's mind. But it all kicked off again the next day when the newspaper article appeared.

This time the call to come straight away for a meeting came from the Secretary of State's office. Will's walk round to that office felt like it took a lot longer than usual and he counted his paces to try to keep himself calm. When he got there, he was greeted not only by his boss but by Sharon Ings, the Permanent Secretary, and also by someone he didn't know.

"Hello, Will," the Secretary of State said in a more formal tone of voice than he normally used for Will. "We need to talk to you about this story that was in the press this morning. And we have been joined by the Department's Head of Security who you may not have met before. Sharon can tell you a bit more."

"Thanks, Secretary of State," Sharon began. "Yes, we have had a formal complaint from the Regulator about the newspaper article. He says it threatens his independence, undermines his ability to regulate the sector, and he wants us to reveal who said those words to the journalist, and demands that we put the record straight that this is not in fact what the Secretary of State thinks. And the Secretary of State has asked me to investigate what has happened here."

"Great," said Will, trying hard to look into Sharon's eyes. No signs of weakness. No signs of guilt. "Sounds like the right thing to do."

What was in her mind? Did she think he would suddenly confess to some indiscretion if she threatened him with the Head of Security? Was she trying to protect her own team by throwing the mantle of suspicion all over him?

Or maybe she was just going through the motions herself?

"So what happens now?" he asked.

"Well, the Head of Security will interview anyone who he thinks may have information on this incident and report to me and I will then report to the Secretary of State."

Will couldn't help feeling tense and he feared it might show. So he tried to change the focus of the conversation. "And what about the 'putting the record straight' idea?" he said, this time talking to his boss, the Secretary of State. "Are you OK with that? The Regulator is not exactly your favourite person."

"We'll see, we'll see," came the evasive answer from the Secretary of State who then asked Will to stay behind for a quick chat.

It was a strange conversation. The Secretary of State clearly did not want to ask if Will was the source.

"This is a bit tricky, Will," he began when all the civil servants had shuffled out. But instead of going into the obvious question he went off in another direction.

"I think it's a clever tactic by the Regulator. This all makes it much harder for us to ease him out of the job. In fact, it's so perfect for him that I would not be surprised if he is not the source of the whole thing."

That seemed unlikely, even to Will, but he could understand the frame of thinking.

Will felt relieved. If he had been asked directly by his boss, he would of course have denied it. But his boss couldn't know what Will would say if he asked and they both would have been in a very awkward position if the answer he got was that Will was the source. Without that question asked, the Secretary of State had perfect deniability, whatever happened. And that of course, as Will knew, was why his boss had not asked him the question.

They went into the area that seemed to concern the Secretary of State more. Should they put out some statement denying these were the Secretary of State's thoughts? Given the earlier discussion, he was clearly not going to be keen on this.

"I suspect you have to," said Will reluctantly. "If you don't, then the implicit suggestion is that you agree with what has been said."

"I know, Will. I know we have to do it. But a lot of our backbenchers won't like it – they always hated him when we were in Opposition and it's got no better since. But it all depends on how I say it. Let's see if we can make it sound like when a football manager gets the dreaded vote of confidence from the board."

The issue was bound to come up in Departmental Oral Questions in the House of Commons scheduled for the following week, where the Opposition spokesman, as well as backbenchers on both sides, got time to ask the Secretary of State virtually anything they wanted. So, Will and the Secretary of State worked on what he would say on this issue. That bit of politics was something Will rather enjoyed.

Meanwhile Will was interviewed by the Head of Security. He had been interviewed in leak enquiries before and he knew they were usually about as far away from a tough interrogation as could be. But he could still feel his body tensing as the interview began.

After the formal bit about the importance of the enquiry, the Head of Security came to the point. "Were you the source for this journalist?"

"No, I was not," answered Will, clear in his own mind by now that whatever he had said to the journalist, he was not the direct source of the kind of inflammatory language that had been used.

"But you do, and you did, speak to the journalist didn't you?"

"Yes, I do," said Will, "as I have said all along. It's part of my job. But the last time was a while back."

"And did you discuss the Secretary of State's views of the Regulator in these conversations?"

This was trickier. What do you say on that one? The truth was complicated – if he even knew what it was.

"Not that I recall," he answered, looking hard at the Head of Security in a way he was sure made him look shifty.

But the Head of Security moved on past the danger point.

"And do you have any knowledge of who the source may be?"

Will was tempted to name half the people he disliked in the Department – and that he thought might be up to something like this. Names flited through his mind, and ways of saying them that pointed towards them but did not directly accuse anyone.

But instead he said, "No idea I'm afraid."

There was a bit of media follow-up to the first press story – but it was only in the business pages and in the specialist press. Nothing to be worried about, and Will could feel the tension ebb away. Except that there was one hurdle yet to come: the ordeal of the Oral Questions.

The House of Commons was made for gladiatorial battle – it was even physically set up to encourage conflict and rancour, with the government and the opposition sides sat opposite and facing down each other, not in a semi-circle as in so many modern parliaments. And the theatricality of the old building added spice to all its goings on.

Will was allowed to be in the officials' box down near the floor of the House for these events and he sometimes liked to go to get a real feel for what the atmosphere was like, to sense the mood of the House. But he'd kept away today and was watching on Parliament TV back in the office. Yet he still felt tense.

These Oral Questions drifted around a bit with one or two specific questions aimed to get their questioner some kudos with their local electorate and media.

But then the Opposition's Shadow Secretary Of State stood up to ask a question. He gave it everything he had.

In a booming and superior voice he began performing, especially to his own backbenchers.

"What we have heard from the coverage in the press shows without doubt that our whole structure of independent regulation, so carefully built up by our Party in government, has been severely damaged by the

Honourable Member who has been busy undermining its very basis. A system admired across the world, that has kept political interference out of regulation, and so has made businesses and consumers more confident that they can trust what the regulator does, and which has given us more investment and lower prices."

He turned to face his opposite number, glaring at him with contempt.

"Will he now apologise and tell us if he still supports our independent energy regulator?"

Will clutched the TV remote very tightly with an intense mixture of anticipation and fear.

The Secretary of State began quietly and in a very controlled manner. "I have the utmost respect for the Regulator who rightly is acting independently and in line with the policies of this democratically elected government."

And then he looked behind him to his own back-benchers, and the tone of his voice changed markedly.

"But I will take no lessons from the Honourable Member opposite about regulation," he thundered. "Under him and his Party, we saw chief executives of privatised utilities lining their pockets, investments not being made, poorer consumers paying more for a unit of energy than rich ones while shareholders made hay." He paused, savouring the brief silence.

"The person that should be apologising to this House for all this damage caused is the Honourable Gentleman himself!"

The Government backbenchers roared with approval. The din was raucous. The danger was over. As far as most people were concerned that was the end of the matter. Will's pulse calmed down. The incident was over and he lived to fight another day.

And the next time Will saw that journalist, neither of them even mentioned it.

Education, Education, Education

Darren had been trying to get the Secretary of State for Education a meeting with the Prime Minister for a couple of weeks but to his increasing frustration, he was getting nowhere. The White Paper to set out the government's schools' agenda was due out in six weeks, but a key element was still unresolved and it needed a meeting to decide it one way or the other. The PM however was very busy and his diary secretary and his closest confidants had been fiercely guarding his diary.

Now, at last, the PM had agreed, and the No.10 Private Office had timetabled the meeting for three days' time. As one of the PM's key policy advisers Darren needed to talk to Steve, the Secretary of State for Education, to see whether he was still on side for what he and Darren had been planning.

A quick bit of texting from Darren – he knew Steve well enough to do that – had found a time they could both do in the half hour before that week's Cabinet meeting in Downing Street the next day. Because it was Cabinet day and various Cabinet Ministers would be knocking around the building, Darren dressed up a bit smarter than usual, with a well-ironed shirt and a tie under his standard charcoal suit. It had amused his partner that morning more used to him setting off for work looking a bit of a scruff.

Meeting a Secretary of State in his own small, shared office in No.10 was unusual – normally advisers went to the Departments to speak to Ministers – but it suited both Darren and Steve's diaries to breach protocol this time.

As he saw Steve he smiled. He liked Steve, he'd worked for Steve in the past and he and his partner had had dinner with Steve once or twice. He also liked the way Steve wore a slightly crumpled blue linen suit, such a different look from the rest of the Cabinet. But Darren groaned when he realised that Steve had brought his special adviser, Emma, along too. He knew that would be trouble. The smartly dressed, thirty-something Emma's politics were different from his and she loved nothing better than getting one over on the Downing Street "machine". Emma's presence would make everything that much harder.

Darren only had one comfortable chair in the room. He offered this battered, but comfortable old green leather chair to Steve, sat behind his desk himself, and let Emma sit herself on the office chair belonging to the other desk that occupied the room.

"So, Steve, have you done any more thinking on the school accountability issue?"

"Yes, Darren, but it's not easy." Steve's tone of voice and his defensive body language reeked of a desire to be somewhere else. Darren knew he had a struggle on his hands if Steve was not to back out.

"I know, I know," Darren responded, trying to sound empathetic. "But I think we need to do it."

"Is the PM up for it?" Steve asked, fiddling with his glasses as he looked at Darren.

Darren hesitated. He knew the PM's agreement was not in the bag at all but if he let on to Steve then Steve's already melting backbone would completely dissolve. And Emma was always sniffing around for signs of weakness.

"I think we can get him on board," Darren said.

Then he knew he needed to remind Steve of what they were doing and why. To get him excited and angry as he knew he could from their previous time working together.

"Steve, you know that if we continue to judge schools purely on the number of kids they manage to get good grades for in the GCSE exams they do at sixteen, then the ones that will always look the best will be the schools with good, middle class, easy-to-teach pupils. The schools that do a phenomenal job with very difficult sets of kids won't get a look in and will be way down the performance league tables." Darren was gently pounding his fists on the desk. This wasn't just an intellectual argument. He knew this really mattered to hundreds of schools, to thousands of children. It had affected the different experiences of school that he and his siblings had enjoyed.

Steve's facial expression suggested that he still agreed with this analysis, so Darren carried on in the same vein.

"So, we need to bring in a measure that holds head teachers accountable on some sort of value-added measure, one that takes account of the abilities and backgrounds of the kids they have to work with. Something that says that what this head has managed to do with some pretty tricky children is actually better than this head with an easy to teach bunch, even though their overall grades were not so good."

He was getting passionate and felt his hackles rising, especially when he caught a glimpse of Emma's ice-cold, sceptical stare. So he tried to tone it down a little, to become more logical.

"Look, we are not suggesting getting rid of the old style 'on-off', 'pass-the-hurdle' measures. As a parent I want to know how many exams the school is getting its pupils through." His children were only in primary school at the moment so it was an easy thing to say. "But we need to give equal billing to a value-added approach. Some kind of approach that says, 'How well does this school do with the raw material it is given?' "

"You know I agree with you, Darren," Steve replied in a conciliatory tone, holding on to his jacket lapel with his fingers as though to steel himself. "I hate seeing schools in my constituency marked down as poor simply because the kinds of families that use them are not ones where children grow up with books in the home." Darren sensed that Steve was becoming animated in spite of himself. And he felt relief that he had punched through to Steve's real feelings here, feelings of anger, so that his natural political caution and calculation were swept aside. His girlfriend always said that passion was Darren's greatest strength – and his greatest weakness.

Steve continued with his passion barely under control. "These families have no expectations of their kids going to university, or even any belief that learning is important. The teachers that dare to teach there do miracles. I know; I've seen it." He pulled his hands through his hair, letting his anger subside. Darren had noticed Emma staring at Steve, as close to open-mouthed as she ever got. Steve, who had a well-earned reputation for keeping calm and level-headed, kept his eyes facing down and raised them only to look at Darren – as though embarrassed to let Emma see so much of his true feelings. She looked over at him with what Darren thought was a look of contempt, and then took refuge by glaring intently at her mobile phone.

Steve sighed and then shrugged. "But it isn't that easy. You and I have been round and around this. You know it and I know it; there are lots of problems and it isn't that simple."

Darren was not giving up. He felt there was still plenty to play for and he felt his heart beat a little stronger. He kept calm but firm. "Nothing worth doing is ever simple," he replied quietly, playing on what he knew Steve's own view of the world was.

"On your advice," continued Steve, putting on his slightly pompous, 'I am the Education Secretary's voice, "I did that long note for the PM – the case for this change, the link to our mission as a government, answers to the

67

objections people have made, even a bloody annex with ways of overcoming the technical measurement issues. And what did I get? Not one bit of feedback in response." Darren was annoyed at this attack on his current boss, and the whining tone that Steve was taking. He was also unable to ignore Steve looking across at Emma's supportive gaze as he got to the end of this oration.

"You know the PM," Darren laughed, although he could tell it sounded a bit forced. "He wants to see where everyone is before he moves." He stared hard at Steve who responded by slowly but deliberately averting his gaze and walking over to the window overlooking Downing Street apparently eager to see what lay outside. Darren knew his next words would be key to the progress of this whole issue. He gave it his best shot – trying to avoid Emma's increasingly hostile stare.

"You know, Steve, what motivates the PM in education has never been about accountability or measuring progress. It's about driving up standards in badly performing schools and tempting the middle classes back into the state system." Darren paused and thought hard. He needed something more, to give Steve confidence that this was all not wasted effort. "So yes, he comes to this issue being a little bit sceptical. But I have spoken to him about this and he asked me to work with you on a viable proposition. And we have one now."

"That's good, Darren, and thanks for that," replied Steve, turning back from his reverie out of the window. "But I'm not sure I believe it really."

"What do you mean?" asked Darren, the tension creeping back into his voice as he wondered if Steve was trying to back out.

"Well the idea that the PM would agree to this – it just does not feel like him," Steve said, gesturing with his arms.

"This whole idea of value-added measures is hard to explain to anyone and it really only appeals to those who already believe in us – not floating voters. And in any case, we can't *prove* that it will make life better for the kids we really care about."

"It's a bit risky, that's true," Darren countered, swivelling on his black, unusually shiny shoes. "And yes, it will be a bit hard to sell to the public. But you know it is the right thing to do and I think we can get the PM there." He pushed on a bit harder. "It is not going to happen though, Steve, unless he really thinks you want it. So are we going to argue for it or not?"

Steve looked anxious – not sure which way to go, trying to catch Emma's eye. Then Emma spoke up. "The teacher unions won't like it," she said quietly but with deadly force and total firmness.

Darren was angry with Emma for stirring it up, even though he knew this point would be made at some stage. There was venom in his tone.

"If we did what the teachers unions wanted, we'd never have had the literacy hour, never had the standardized tests that help us map how kids are doing, never had a target to reduce the number of failing schools." It was over the top but Darren needed to argue hard to see off Emma. Darren knew she was close to Steve. She had worked for him in different jobs now for three years after cutting her teeth in the main public sector trade union. And she was good at her job.

"Anyway," continued Darren, softening his tone just a little but keeping the pressure up, "why would school leaders be against this? It's surely fairer than what we have at present."

Emma came straight back at Darren, the deliberate calmness and evenness in her voice more devastating than if she had thrown emotion into it. "It's just another addition of more and more complex rules and monitoring. More intrusive bureaucracy aimed at keeping an eye on the person doing their best at the front of the class. It goes against everything teachers and their unions believe as professionals." She held a stare for a moment, letting her words sink in. Darren knew this was a calculated move, letting the thought linger, aimed at making Steve think and worry, and judging by Steve's anxious face, it had begun to work. Darren felt himself starting to sweat. "Yes, you're right, Darren," Emma said with the smile of the chess master knowing they have made a good move, "the teachers can be obstructive and just defend their patch at times; but I don't think you can argue that they are wrong on this one."

Darren was not prepared to accept that. He needed to draw on that passion again. Trying to hold back too much of the anger that was brewing in him he put his case firmly. "But some form of added value measure must be better than the crude league tables that we have now that push teachers to ignore the child who is easily going to get the five good GCSEs or who is never going to get them and focus on pushing a small number over that threshold."

"Yes," answered Emma, equally firmly, "but they would prefer no league tables at all."

Well we're not having that, Darren thought to himself, but was careful to avoid saying it.

Steve listened. He sighed and fiddled with his glasses again.

"Darren, you are pretty keen on this stuff. And so am I and I would go for it too if I thought it were possible with everything considered. But Emma makes good points." He put his hands up in a gesture of despair and then collapsed them down to his sides again. Darren could sense the calculations going on in Steve's head as he tried to negotiate the territory, stuck between these two advisers, one his own, one the PM's, both of whom he knew well. "Listen, I'll give it a go tomorrow with the PM. But if it doesn't fly, I'm not dying in a ditch. We have plenty of other things in this White Paper that work for me."

Darren wasn't really surprised that this was the stance Steve was taking. In fact, to get him to say he would argue, in front of the PM, for this policy that Darren so believed in, was quite an achievement. Darren knew that. But he was also frustrated and angry.

Steve must know this had to be the right policy. Why was he backing off now? They had all worked for years, decades even, to be in power, to make a difference so that all those kids that started off the race of life with a big disadvantage got a fair chance. What was the point of being in power if the difficult issues were always just ducked, if the path of least resistance was always taken? If you didn't do what was right but only what was easily achievable?

But Darren knew that this was nonsense. He wasn't an idealist, a utopian. Compromises had to be made. Battles had to be won in stages. Allies had to be brought along. Every step in the right direction was an achievement and going for broke with brave "revolutionary" fervour got you nowhere. It could make you feel good but if you didn't win and stay in power there was not much you could do for the kids he wanted to help.

On this issue though, Darren was dug in very deep.

He was not just arguing from a sense of logic and good policy making but from a deep well of passion and anger. He had always had a fury about seeing schools who could easily recruit good pupils lauded above those who did pretty well even against the odds. It came from his childhood when he saw the unfairness of it all. Not for him – he had gone to a "good" school – but for his sister who

71

was at a perfectly good school but one that middle class parents would not look at. More recently, much of that feeling had come rushing back in a visit to a school as part of his job. He had seen a dedicated head and hard-working committed teachers doing their very best yet unable to force this "doomed" school up the attainment league tables and derided because of it. How did that make the kids feel? How did that motivate teachers? How did that help the local community?

But he wasn't going to win this one on raw emotion. It was far more complex than that.

The problem in getting Steve on board, Darren knew, was nothing to do with his deep beliefs – they were in the right place – but that Steve knew that he had serious adversaries on this. Some of them were in his very own Education department where the senior civil servants saw this policy as an old chestnut beloved of technical experts and economists but one that would never fly. They had seen off this sort of idea a number of times before and they certainly weren't making it easy or arguing the case for it across Whitehall on the civil service "net" in the way that Steve needed.

But worse, Darren knew that a number of Steve's colleagues – other Cabinet members – were not on board and Steve was fully aware of that too. If he was to get this through he needed to construct some alliances and he needed to work out how to do this fast.

The meeting broke up with both men agreeing to test out the lay of the land a bit more. Darren felt he was agreeing to see how to overcome any opposition, but he feared that Steve, with the encouragement of Emma, would be looking for further reasons to back out. But that was as far as Darren could get at this point. Darren's next move was to give

Mark White a ring to see if he was free for a chat. Mark was the private secretary to the PM, one of the civil servants who worked closely with him on a day-to-day basis and covered a number of departments including Education. He was a smart official, in his mid-thirties, who had worked in several other departments and was clearly going to go on to higher things. They agreed to meet for a coffee in the tiny No.10 canteen.

Mark did not bring good news. He was in and around the PM all day, picking up on his moods and concerns, but also on what other ministers were saying.

"Truth is, Darren, that there are not a lot of supporters for this."

Jesus Christ, Darren thought. *The fuckers.*

"But are people hostile or just not very bothered?" Darren asked, looking for scraps of good news. He knew the difference between outright hostility and lack of enthusiasm. With the latter he could work; with the former it would be a trial of strength.

"Well, I guess the problem you have here is that most departments don't care at all."

"Not that much of a problem," grinned Darren, "as long as they keep out of it." But he knew that was a bit desperate. He needed some political support.

"You've got the Cabinet Office behind you," continued Mark, "because the minister there has responsibility for social mobility and he sees this as being useful."

"And he is a bit of a policy wonk," laughed Darren.

"And that too," Mark agreed, with a wry smile.

"The local government department have got involved," Mark continued. "They've gone for a formal 'concerned that this policy will add to the costs for local government if they have to administer it and deal with schools' as their Minister's answer."

Darren groaned. "That will have been drafted by good old, ultra-cautious civil servants who focus on the minor costs to their department of an idea, not the meaning of it or the point of principle."

"Maybe," said Mark giving nothing away. He was, after all, a career civil servant himself. Nevertheless, at this minute his refusal to commit or show some feelings annoyed Darren right through.

"Anyway it's not that bad. I checked up directly with the Secretary of State for Local Government and she told me she can support the idea if she is convinced it leads to a system that stops what she sees as discrimination in the league table system against areas with poorer, less easy populations. It's just that she wants some more resource to pay for the extra work needed."

"That's good news," said Darren, wanting to punch the air. "Always knew that Chris would 'get' this," he said.

"Hang on though, Darren. She then went on to give a lot of concerns as to whether this could ever work."

"OK," said Darren, a bit deflated. He could hardly argue with the thought that actually making all this work would be difficult as it needed all sorts of data to be available and to be adjusted correctly. But he knew that to have a chance he needed Christine to join with Steve to increase the pressure on the doubters.

"That the sum of it?" Darren asked.

"Formally, yes," said Mark. "As I said, most departments did not register a view. But I think the gremlins are getting at your idea."

"What gremlins?" Darren asked, with a sense of foreboding creeping through his body. He was pretty sure he knew what Mark meant.

"Well, when the PM was having his catch up with Julian the other day, Julian threw in a very Julian-type aside about this." Darren felt his chest tightening; if the PM's closest political ally was getting involved, the stakes were definitely that much higher. "Julian," Mark continued, "said that Steve was a good Minister, re-building the education system, doing really good work on the things that matter to parents and voters like discipline, truanting and a focus on the 3Rs, but that he was getting distracted by an idea that would only confuse people and achieve little." Darren felt his shoulders drop and his suit jacket suddenly feel very heavy on them.

Mark's summary did not sound good. Julian was one of the PM's key confidantes, an MP with a roving brief in the government to spot booby traps, and to keep everybody in tune with where the public, the voters, were heading. He was a good guy, Julian, and Darren got on with him well. He was a real believer in doing good. But he also wanted to be re-elected to do more good and Darren and he did not always see eye to eye on what that meant. And crucially in a fight for the ear of the PM, Darren knew who would win – and it wasn't him.

"Julian would say that I guess," said Darren with a sigh, "but he doesn't know the full story yet."

Mark was not finished with the tricky news. "And then you have the two former Secretaries of State for Education who are still in the Cabinet doing different jobs now, who have rejected this sort thing in their time at the department and are not likely to change now," added Mark.

"Great," murmured Darren, trying to keep the dejection out of his voice.

"And you have the Chair of the Education Select Committee who hates league tables anyway and keeps telling the PM that."

"Helpful stuff," Darren said sarcastically. He looked down at his hands and sighed.

He was depressed. He'd more or less suspected everything that Mark had now told him. The task ahead of him was very daunting – maybe impossible. He had to give it a go, but the odds had shortened markedly. Nevertheless, he was not going to give up. He owed it to all the children out there, about to be failed by the stupid system of assessment, to try as hard as he could.

"I think we should get a note to the PM tonight about this. And can you grab me twenty minutes for a pre-meeting with him tomorrow?"

"Already done on the meeting," said Mark, "although you know very well that he is likely to overrun the defence and security meeting scheduled before so I doubt you will get any time with him directly before that. And I will draft a note for him for the main meeting and let you see it before I give it to him."

"Mark," Darren asked, "what do you think? Am I crazy to push this?"

"Well, I'm a civil servant, Darren." He looked hard but kindly at Darren as though trying to work out the right words to use. "I think you are up against it and you have to work out how much you are going to risk pushing for it."

Darren grimaced and he felt his gut turning over. In civil servant speak, what Mark had said was as close to a "you haven't got a cat in hells chance" as you ever got.

"On the substance though," Mark continued, getting into his stride, "you have to be right – in theory at least. But would it drive performance and behaviour in ways you want? I think the jury is pretty much out on that."

Darren knew that Mark had raised a legitimate issue – but waiting to try and prove it in the abstract was not part of his strategy. If he never got this bloody thing through nobody would ever know if it would have worked. And it certainly could not make things worse.

He thanked Mark, and then considered his options as he wandered back upstairs to his office. How best to make this a puzzle where all the parts would, at a stroke, fit into place? He could concentrate on tightening up the arguments or he could work on Steve some more, or he could try something else. He pondered a little and decided the priority had to be to find some solid allies. That meant getting Chris, the Secretary of State for Local Government, fully on board. She could be the person that gave strength to the argument and stopped it just looking like a Steve – and Darren – obsession.

He managed to get Christine on the phone the next day after a bit of leaning on her private office to find the time. She listened but she would not commit. Darren became increasingly frustrated. "Come on, Christine, this is a good policy for you in trying to help revive communities that are in trouble. And you know it's right."

"Darren, I admire your energy on this. Yes, it would help but it puts no new money my way, and it does not help me get these kids better schools or teachers. It just can't be a priority for me." As ever, Darren acknowledged wryly to himself, money was the currency that really mattered in these power games.

"Chris, I need you. Steve needs you."

Darren could hear a shrug in Christine's voice. She was a decent woman, an ex-teacher, on the modernising wing of the Party. "I will do what I can but I am not sticking my neck too far out on this."

Darren had done what he could with her. How Christine would play it as negotiations went on was unclear, but if she felt a bit of wind behind the policy she might just deliver. But more bits of the jigsaw needed to be put together to make that happen.

Darren knew he needed the communications part of the

No.10 machine on board – or at last not openly hostile – if the PM was to be convinced. So he phoned Rick, part of the comms team who always had a good feel about how the place was likely to react to new ideas. A fellow political *apparatchik*, he was always up for bold ideas, but never afraid to call time when the politics did not add up. So Darren was optimistic that Rick would help him out with at least a steer one way or the other.

"So you've got some good material for this White Paper," Rick began in his slightly Brummy accent. "Steve and you have done well. It's got several days' worth of stories. Stuff for the popular papers, stuff for the commentariat. It shows our direction, our purpose. It shows momentum."

Ah yes, momentum: the key watchword for the comms team. Ever show you had come to a halt, and you were mincemeat in their eyes. So, permanent revolution – often driving teachers and other public sector workers to despair. One person's momentum was another's initiative-overload.

Trouble was that many of his policy colleagues agreed. Keep pushing, keep occupying the territory, keep advancing on. Even worse, the PM sort of agreed too.

Darren was sure the issue of accountability was going to feel pretty trivial in the scheme of things to Rick.

"But what's the one liner about it then, Darren? You care a lot about this, so explain its importance in a sound bite."

At the back of his mind Darren had known that Rick would ask him this. And he knew he did not really have an answer. He was furious at himself for not being better prepared. He stared into his mug of coffee, looking for inspiration, hesitating before speaking down the phone.

"It's about putting a spotlight on what schools and their heads are actually achieving so we can judge the good schools from the bad. So we can learn what works and what doesn't, so we spread good practice." Even as Darren said it, he knew it sounded dry, without emotion. Something he knew would go down well in one of the think-tanks he had worked in in the past but would leave the key voter focus groups as cold and uninspired as a Tesco "value" frozen lasagne.

"OK, I'll go with you for the moment," said Rick helpfully. He and Darren had worked together for a number of years so there was some trust there. Darren smiled weakly and said, "Thanks Rick" in a quiet voice. He felt grateful but embarrassed that he needed this help.

"So," began Rick, "is it 'New system to help parents choose the best schools for their kids'?"

Darren thought hard. That would be a decent top line. He liked it and he felt his heart beat a little faster. He nearly said yes. But he hesitated because it wasn't quite right.

Was he really suggesting that parents send their kids to a school that got very few kids getting five good grades in the GCSE exams but did a terrific job in getting at least some exam passes for difficult children from deprived backgrounds – because that was the thing this value added measure tried to assess. Would that really be the only basis upon which he made decisions for his kids? He knew it wasn't. This inconsistency made him feel uncomfortable, not knowing which way to turn.

He stared vacantly out of the window for a second or two with his mobile glued to his ear, then began again. "It's sort of that Rick, but I need to think about it."

"OK, Darren, OK." Rick made a sigh that Darren suspected was the beginnings of exasperation. The sigh said what Darren knew: that it was a bit late in the day to not know what the overwhelming, "easy to understand" reason for this policy was.

He also knew that if he couldn't explain it simply then it would never really have the bite and impact on teachers, parents and schools that he hoped it might. This wasn't just about PR.

"Rick, I need help here. It's sort of ending the perverse incentives that having a target of five good GCSEs that you either get and are 'good' or don't and are 'bad' gives. It's making every child count and be valued – even if they are never going to pass the threshold. It's stopping a bias against working class schools."

Darren had been in full flight there. But the response from Rick took what felt like an age. "All good motives," said Rick eventually. "But it doesn't 'roll off the tongue' does it, mate?"

Darren sighed, looked down, and racked his brain. Then he got up and paced the room, clutching the mobile to his ear. He was not going to let go of this because he did not have a catchy enough sound bite. "Does it matter if there is no strong, easy line? If it's just a technical policy change among a lot of big-ticket changes?"

"Look, Darren, you may be right. But I think you'll find that not everyone feels like that." Rick hesitated, and Darren felt there was some bad news coming. There was. "Carl is out to get this," said Rick quietly.

Not bloody Carl, thought Darren. *That is all I need.*

Carl was another comms person but a much more day-to-day operator who focussed on the difficult world of the Tory-leaning tabloids. "He's deeply suspicious of such a wonk heavy policy and he thinks it plays straight into the dumbing down story the tabs always want to play about us and education…"

"Oh, for Christ's sake, Rick."

"Just telling you, Darren. So you need to counter him. Julian will listen to Carl."

Darren knew that was true and he also knew that Carl and Emma were good friends. He feared the worst.

Darren had done as much due diligence as he could. But he felt uncomfortable, unfulfilled and his stomach churned away. His battalions were just not in the right place.

The big meeting took place the next day.

About twenty minutes before the time of the meeting with the PM the forces started to gather. All the attendees were government people – from No.10 and the Education department – so nobody was waiting in the designated waiting room but had all wandered around to the press area, not far from the PM's office.

This was a place Darren did not often go, the sanctuary of the press office, the place the strategic comms brigade and the spinners hung out.

Darren had some brief, civil words with Carl and Rick. He was pretty nervous and he knew they could all see that. Slowly everyone assembled.

Some of the cast were civil servants, including Mark, the private secretary, but the heavyweight players were the political appointees. Of them, most were media people but there were some strategy and policy colleagues as well.

The mood was not good. Darren reckoned that most of them thought this was a daft and irrelevant debate that was wasting some of their precious time and he could see signs of irritation on the faces of many of his colleagues. Darren knew he had done his preparation and that others probably had not. But he also knew that it was going to be him – and Steve – having to prove the case with others trying to knock it down. He did not resent that – it was sort of their job after all. But it made him feel he was being ganged up on, as though he were the kid at school surrounded by shouting and jabbing children. And he sort of hoped the teacher would turn up to tell them all to be nice.

Darren badly wanted to get a few words with the PM

before the meeting. As the PM's adviser on education, he was usually allowed that. But as had been predicted, the previous meeting was running over. Mark had said he would call him in when the PM was ready, but nothing was happening.

So Darren wandered over to loiter outside the PM's Office.

After a few minutes he saw those from the previous meeting come out of the room. He could tell by the uniforms that there were some generals, and he recognised the Secretary of State for Defence and the guys in No.10 who did the defence and secret service stuff – people he did not see that often and quite frankly didn't really understand.

He knew that the PM usually liked a few minutes to calm down and re-adjust from one meeting before getting thrown into the next and that his main concern was usually what had been happening in the world while he had been locked away. So engaging him straight away always had risks but he had no alternative if this meeting was going to have a chance of going the way Darren wanted it to.

So as the others trooped out Darren trooped in.

He tried with a bit of small talk first to bridge the gap.

"Looks like that was a heavy-duty meeting."

"Yeah," said the PM, a big man with a hangdog look, "those guys are always so hard to read. The agendas they come with make the Party debates look tame." The PM looked pretty tired, his tie slightly undone, his hair a bit bedraggled.

"Prime Minister, may I just give you a quick brief on your next meeting."

"Oh Christ, do I get no break at all?" the PM moaned, in the style of a troublesome teenager. "This office, they think I just want meetings on top of meetings."

"It's about the Education White Paper, PM. You know,

I did you a note about it last week and Mark gave you an update note last night."

"Yes, OK, Darren, I'll get into it."

"Prime Minister, I just want to alert you to the point of contention, the reason we need a meeting with you."

"Look, I read the paper. It is something to do with changing the way you decide a good school. Not sure on it, let's hear what everyone has to say."

"Yes, but Prime Minister—"

"I'm not sure why we are having the meeting – it all sounded OK to me. Is anyone disagreeing?"

"Some are disagreeing, Prime Minister. That is why we need the meeting. Me and Steve want some change and a lot of the rest of the team do not."

"OK, OK," the PM replied in an offhand tone, his hands waving around but his attention wavering.

Darren could feel a lack of engagement from the PM, a lack that might cost him dear in the denouement of this whole process. On the other hand, he was up on where he might have been since the PM thought his proposal "sounded OK". He had to make a quick decision with the last few words he was going to get here. He went for playing a cautious card to try to ensure that if the meeting went wrong he could live to fight another day.

"Prime Minister, my advice would be that unless you are certain we should do it, don't decide anything at this meeting." But he wasn't being heard and he knew it.

He did not get a chance to talk any more as the PM stuck his head out of the door and hollered across to one of his press aides.

"Carl, anything happen with the article we are trying to place in the *Wall Street Journal* – has the President agreed to do a joint one?"

He was off on a different track. Darren had lost him.

Now he was going to be on his own – perhaps with some support from a nervous Steve – and would just have to do whatever he could in the meeting.

After a short delay, the education meeting began in the PM's Office. Darren took his seat quickly and then watched the other players file in, a few silent, a few chatting away, a few with coffee cups, and a few with papers. They then distributed themselves as if following the stage directions of some well-loved, familiar play. The key seats were the two armchairs facing the PM's armchair, reserved, as was the unspoken tradition, for the key politicians. Darren sat just to the side of them as befitted his role as a non-elected but key adviser, and with an ability to catch the eye of the PM. Most of the rest of the cast sat further back behind the armchairs. Emma was back there with a look of thunder in her face, and Sarah was present as the senior member of the press team along with the redoubtable Carl and the friendlier face of Rick. Mark, the private secretary sat a bit further back still, there to make sure the PM was OK and to take a note of the meeting.

One of the armchairs was taken by Steve as was his right as Secretary of State, the other, at the beginning, was left vacant. Everyone knew who that was for. And right on cue Julian marched in just as the meeting was about to begin. As ever with Julian, it was the entrance of someone who knew they were important, smart dressed with an element of class that most of the rest of them did not have. Not until he had settled in and had made a bit of small talk with Steve and the PM, did they get down to business.

Darren could feel the tension rising in him, a clamminess attacking his palms. He wondered how he would do. It wasn't simple nerves, for he had been at many crucial meetings before and could hold his own. No, it was because here he was after something he really wanted, really felt mattered to so many children and their families and yet he knew he was almost entirely alone. He doubted himself. He did not know if he could pull it off. But he had to go for it.

So at the invitation of the PM, Darren started his pitch. A bit of detail and history, a bit of those for and against it among stakeholders, and a bit about how he thought it could be sold to the general public. He caught an encouraging smile from Rick. As far as he could tell, surveying his audience, he had at least got them listening. Some were glancing at their BlackBerrys and texting on their phones but that was par for the course. Darren's presentation was all done in a matter of minutes – he knew the PM looked tired and a bit ratty so going on for any length of time would do him no good. Darren felt he'd done all right – the case was good, the reasons for doing it clear and he had had a bash at how they might present it. Maybe it would go the way he wanted after all.

Darren now passed the baton to Steve. He needed a good leg from Steve – the race was there to be won.

But while Steve said the right things, he was clearly not putting his neck on the line on this one.

"Darren's outlined the position well. I think there's real merit in the idea so I hope you can agree to it, Prime Minister. I know there are some issues on the comms side, but I am pretty sure we can overcome them." It sounded fine, but Darren feared that the others would have heard Steve's lack of conviction or passion. It certainly annoyed Darren who could see rats deserting what might be a sinking ship – even before it had left the harbour.

In the way of these things, the opposition started off gently, feeling their way.

Sarah, said, "Tricky sell – complicated and no real pitch to a guttural emotion that parents might have. We'd have to work very hard on the language."

Then Darren felt the atmosphere heading for a more difficult level as Carl came in with, "And, Emma, am I right the teachers are hostile?"

Emma piled in. With relish. "They are very hostile. Maybe they are being too defensive, but they've had a lot thrown at them in recent years and at some point we will have pushed them over the edge." Without ever really trashing the position her boss was taking, or appearing to contradict him, she made it sound like only rejection of this wild proposal would stop an all-out strike.

Quite ludicrous in Darren's view but he kept to the point as he retaliated.

"We can get others out there welcoming it – the heads like it, the academics are up for it and I know that Fred Smithson, the old Ofsted boss, will support us."

At this point the PM slightly randomly looked through his papers, a habit that Darren was familiar with and that he knew he used to give himself thinking time.

"Mark," the PM asked his private secretary after a few moments, "who supports this? All the Cabinet on board?"

"Some, Prime Minister," Mark answered, too honestly for Darren's taste. "The Secretary of State for Local Government is pretty much pro, as long as she gets some funding to pay for it, and nobody is strongly against. But there are certainly a good few concerns."

"That isn't too bad – it sounds OK to me." The PM looked round the room as though pleased he had gone with Darren and happy to move on to whatever other duties lay ahead of him.

To Darren's amazement, he was winning and his heart skipped just a little. He could see out of the corner of his eye panic in Emma's eyes just as he noticed a very slight look of surprise and delight in Steve's. An odd pair indeed.

But all was not yet done. Now, the powerful and clever

Julian was preparing to launch himself into the debate. After a magisterial look around the room, catching everybody's eye, he focussed back again at the PM and began to speak.

"Prime Minister, I think Steve and Darren have done a terrific job." Having got everyone's attention, Julian kept silent for a moment, indicating that his words were just a prelude. Darren could sense that all eyes were glued on Julian, tantalised, waiting to find out what was to come. "I think what they are trying to do is admirable. Lots of thought. Lots of intelligence. Lots even, dare I say, it, of elegance."

This was all too nice. The "but" was going to be big and Darren felt his heart beat faster as he prepared for the worst.

"But," he said, throwing his arms wide, "I don't think the time is opportune." He looked at the PM as if to check the PM was really hooked. Then he continued.

"At the moment everything we know about the mood of the electorate says, don't be too clever. We need to respond to what people care about and do it in language they understand."

He turned round to Julie who led on polling. "Isn't that true, Julie?" he asked rhetorically.

Now that everyone knew where Julian was going, one group at the meeting became more relaxed and looked to come in behind him. Darren felt his stomach fall, heavily, to the ground.

The first of the cowardly mob to come in behind Julian's covering fire was Carl. Darren seethed at the mere sound of his voice.

"Actually, I've already had a couple of the political lobby journalists ring me up asking whether it is true that we want to go soft on poor schools by letting them do some adjustment to their results to make them look better." Carl looked straight at the PM as if knowing this was what was needed to encourage him to hammer down on the stake being placed at the heart of this idea. And then with a slight laugh in his voice he banged in hard. "A 'poor head teacher's charter' one called it."

If the content of this attack, cowardly in the extreme by using probably made up third parties to mount the attack, had not been enough, Carl's knowing, half-laugh at the end really got under Darren's skin.

Darren was furious. What the hell was this? Who the hell was leaking to the press – could it really be Emma? Surely, too much for her. Maybe Department officials? He would not put that past some of them. And how dare Carl bring this up now.

He wanted to scream, to swear, to demand fairness. But he held his cool. Instead he tried to be statesmanlike. He needed Steve to come in and support him. He absolutely had to have that support. The Prime Minister would think twice if his own Cabinet Minister fought hard for the idea. The years he and Steve had worked together in the past had to count for something now – surely. He tried to make eye contact with Steve but Steve was having none of it.

To Darren's intense disappointment, Steve kept his counsel and so Darren felt he had to fill the void.

"Look," he said in desperation, "there will of course be people who don't like this, who wantonly misunderstand it. But we can deal with them, we can nuance the proposal, we can get the comms right. We really can."

There was a silence; an uncomfortable silence.

The PM looked at Steve.

"Steve, do you want this? Do we need it? Do we need it now?"

Steve looked round the room. Darren could feel him weighing up the options. Keep going and make an enemy of Julian – a dangerous enemy. And the press boys would give him precious little help. Stop and he looked foolish for letting it get this far. And to add to all that, the look Steve shot across at him made Darren feel that Steve knew that to backtrack would be to have let Darren down big time.

"Prime Minister," began Steve, "I believe in this policy. I've worked with Darren to put it together. It will make the lives of thousands of kids better." He sounded like he cared; like he felt passionately about the importance of this bill. Did this mean he was going to follow through? Darren hoped, even prayed that it would.

"But we don't have to do it now. I can see it could distract us. So it's your call, Prime Minister."

So the white flag had been raised. All Steve's big talk before was just a technique to make him sound "bigger" as he capitulated. Darren felt hurt, let down; but much worse, he felt betrayed. And he felt he was failing.

Darren could see the PM's face relax. He knew the PM was grateful for Steve's volte face which meant that that he would not need to choose amongst his courtiers and that a fight could be avoided. And Darren knew the PM would have calculated that he, Darren, would be angry and upset but that that was manageable and anyway Darren was always loyal.

Darren noticed with contempt that the PM made sure he avoided catching his eye as he spoke.

"I like the policy. I want it worked up. I want plans for selling it discussed and I want you to help with that, Julian. I want you to float it, gently, in a speech, Steve." That was the positive, softening up stuff. Now came the truth. "But we won't put it in the White Paper at the moment."

The meeting broke up. It was over and the whole caravan moved on. Darren was bitterly disappointed and felt personally let down. The whole process was galling, the outcome way below what he thought they could and should have done. But he was a pro, a loyal worker and not just a dreamer. So Darren put his back into getting the rest of that White Paper into as good a shape as could be and turning it into pretty decent legislation. But his particular idea never went anywhere. It died that day.

He asked himself whether he had played his hand as well as he could have. Whether he had wasted a chance to take advantage of this amazing position he was in to try to do something worthwhile, to help the children that he knew needed it. To stop what his sister had had to go through happening to anyone else's sister.

He knew it was like that in the real world of politics; risks too high, so opportunities foregone, rightly or wrongly. Complex ideas ditched in favour of ones that resonate on the doorstep. Decisions made on the basis of the power of the court around the PM not necessarily on objective grounds. He knew it, but sometimes it was hard.

The Chancellor

I had only been working for the Chancellor of the Exchequer for a few months when all hell erupted. Well, maybe not all hell, but certainly a pretty vigorous debate amongst his advisers as to how to handle his latest idea.

Sarah Wild, a long-time advisor and friend to the Chancellor, had brought the news to a meeting of what was termed his Council of Economic Advisers, a six-strong group that I had recently been brought in to be the Chair of. She wore a dark brown trouser suit and oozed authority. She was a nice lady but tough as they come when she wanted to be.

"So," she began, with a quizzical smile and a knowing tone of voice, "he wants us to work up ideas for raising the income level at which people start to pay tax. He thinks it would be a great thing to announce in the Budget."

There was a rather stunned silence.

Sarah's eyes scanned the high-ceilinged, rather functional Treasury room that we used for Council meetings. Not in a "daring you to disagree" way but with the authority of someone who knew that while she may not know as much about economics, or polling, or media handling as the rest of the team, she was very much the senior player here.

I was itching to say something and felt my stomach turn with nervousness and anticipation. If anyone had looked hard they would have seen my index finer banging softly against my mouth.

I did not like the idea of raising tax thresholds at all. I'd looked enough at this sort of thing in the past to know it was expensive and badly targeted at getting money to the poorest in society. A lot of the cash went to the better off while the really poor did not pay income tax so it didn't help them.

But I was the newish boy in the team and I didn't want to sound critical – at least not before some of the rest of the Council had been. So I sat and kept quiet and stared hard down at my notebook.

I was pretty sure most of my colleagues would have doubts – even if they were likely to express them a bit subtly. And the slightly ironic tone Sarah had used to explain all this made it clear that she was a little sceptical too.

But the first response was from Jonathan, and it was no surprise that he wanted to support the boss.

"Well, I can see a lot in that idea," he began. "We'd need to get the details right so we don't end up spending a lot on something that doesn't do much to help the poorer parts of society. But if we can do that, well it looks pretty good to me."

Across the room there was the sound of papers being shuffled and pens being fiddled with. My glimpse at Sarah suggested she had the beginnings of a scowl on her face. We all liked Jonathan even though he was a little different from the rest of us with his three-piece suit and his crisp, well-ironed shirts. He had given up a pretty lucrative career in the City to come and work for the Chancellor a couple of years ago and understood worlds foreign to the rest of us. But his gratefulness at being allowed into this political world by the Chancellor had made him want to be ultra-loyal and unquestioning. And taking on Sarah, even in this gentle way, was a dangerous game to engage in.

I had had some long chats with Jonathan when I first arrived to work at the Treasury. They had been quite intense, more than I really felt comfortable with. He'd explained to me that at times he felt isolated. He knew that when the Chancellor proposed something they didn't like the smell of, a lot of the team ignored it, hoping it would just go away. There wasn't the capacity to pursue all of his whims and some sort of sifting system was needed: most of them reckoned the best bet was to leave the more questionable ones be and only go back to them if the Chancellor's interest continued.

Jonathan, in contrast, tried his best to see if he could get virtually every idea to work. He felt he owed the Chancellor that as he'd taken him on when many in the political world were not keen. But at times, he confessed to me, he found working in this way made him feel very alone. Despite his outward hardness, he didn't want to be seen as separate from the rest of the team, didn't want to get into a fight with anyone, especially Sarah, in some sort of long-term adviser versus new favourite battle. Sometimes, this tension all erupted with him lambasting some junior Treasury staff member for a slightly less than perfect piece of work. I understood where Jonathan was coming from, but a good advisor has to say no to the boss sometimes.

I wasn't sure how to dissolve the awkward atmosphere and I looked somewhat desperately around at my colleagues searching for the right thing to say.

I was supposed in some way to chair this collection of advisors, having been brought in when the previous post holder had left to fight for a Parliamentary seat. It was an honour to take on the job and I felt so proud and pleased when I was offered it. But I also started to sleep badly, wondering whether I was up to it. It was a hard job anyway but even harder because almost all of the current team knew the Chancellor much better than me. True, I had worked with the now Chancellor almost a decade ago so I knew his habits at least a bit and I knew Sarah from those old Opposition days. But that was all historic. So there was an art in managing them, let alone him, and I wasn't sure how to do it, how to lead without pissing off any of his experienced team.

Now I could sense the danger of getting caught between Jonathan and the rest on this issue – especially Sarah. I thought of trying to crack a joke about the art of the possible but thought better of it.

Luckily another member of the team took the conversation off in a way we could all live with. "We need to look at the polling numbers and give him some sort of reflection on how it might play."

That was Sunil. Good old Sunil with his baby face, lovely smile and casual dress sense. Quiet, studious, and unassuming, Sunil was the member of the team who kept tabs on public opinion and helped frame the overall communications strategy. He knew that the Chancellor went through phases like this and he'd told me that the best way to counter them was sometimes to convince him it gave out the wrong narrative; would not play well with the public. That, more than the charts and analysis some of the rest of us would leap to, could be the most effective tool to put the brakes on a bad policy thought of his. Sarah knew that even more.

"That's a good idea, Sunil," I began, grasping desperately at something that avoided being for or against the Chancellor's idea. I needed some space to mull it all over and I hoped maybe this was just another idea he would go cold on soon. But I had to say something more positive too.

"Well, we'd better do some work to scope this – what options are there, how much do they cost, who is affected, how might we present this policy?" This sounded too strong, taking us down the wrong path. I didn't want the team to think I was really up for it. So I smiled and added a rider. "Let's not spend ages on it at this stage – just some first runs at the issues so we can present it all to the boss and take it from there."

"OK," said Sarah, catching me with a firm look, "but we need to get that done pretty fast. At the moment he is quite serious about this."

We all knew what she meant: don't dick around here just hoping it goes away. Jonathan added a bit more in the same vein: "Shall we reconvene on Friday to see where we have got to?" I could hardly disagree but added "...but don't let it get in the way of all the other work being done."

Over the next few days, I knew we had to get under the skin of this tax-cut idea. And I needed to find a strategy to keep the team from fighting each other and to keep the Chancellor happy. Analysis was commissioned, draft papers were produced, small meetings with officials were held. A few, very trusted outsiders were consulted.

I worked closely with the Treasury officials to work out what it might cost, who it made better off and who gained little, if at all, under different options. That was fun, less driven by personalities and politics. The Treasury officials were smart, willing, fast workers, not frightened of working with political appointees, quite different to some of the officials I had worked with as a special adviser in other departments. But they were also pretty young and inexperienced, very fixated on what basic economics told you to do, not what was practical, might work, might be part of a decent political narrative.

I made sure other members of the team were focussed on the areas where they could add value. Sunil had a look at the data on public attitudes and put some ideas into the focus groups that were being used in the run up to the Budget. Most crucially he spent some time trying to put this potential tax change into a comms narrative that sounded consistent with what this redistributionalist Chancellor's previous three years in office had been about. Sarah gently

95

sounded out what No.10 might think of such a move so at least we would know if it would be the beginning of a fight. Jonathan had tested City opinion and thought about what the international markets might think of this move. Others looked at the interaction with welfare benefits and at the fiscal implications. It was a lot of work and it all weighed heavily on my mind.

We reconvened as a group back in the meeting room on the Friday to see where we were. As I knew, Fridays were when the Chancellor went back to his constituency for the weekend and the atmosphere in the Treasury building became significantly more relaxed. It was the day that I could usually get home at a sensible time to see the family.

I came into the room clutching a mug of strong black coffee. It wasn't a meeting I was looking forward to and I didn't really have a plan as to how I wanted it to go. The undercurrents at play emerged pretty fast. In one camp were most of us who wanted to show that this was not a great idea through the power of the various numbers and the feedback on public opinion we had assembled. Jonathan was in a very different camp. In a determined way with his fingers tucked into the little pockets in his waistcoat, and his brow heavily furrowed, he emphasised everything that supported such a change, arguing that the costs were being exaggerated and that the questions used in the polling were loaded. It was pretty strong but when I glanced at Sarah screwing up her face, I felt a sense of relief that he had badly overplayed his hand.

Whatever the differences of opinion I had to keep things moving. Sarah made clear that this idea was still very much in the Chancellor's mind and was not going away. I thought she was still saying it with a sense of regret but I was worried that I was just hearing what I wanted to hear. She played a mean poker hand.

"We need to put the facts and the risks to the Chancellor by the middle of the next week," I said. When I spotted Jonathan's rather vexed face I hurriedly added, "And the opportunities of course."

I was getting a sweat at night when I thought of this. I wanted to kill the idea and I knew Sunil did too. But Jonathan was fighting for it, and Sarah was not giving me clear signs of what she would support. And what about the boss himself? It went round and around in my head and my stomach. In typical fashion I buried myself in analysis to escape from having to focus on this dilemma.

So I worked with the Chancellor's private office over the next few days to make sure we could have a good set of papers and presentations when we met with him to discuss it all. I knew that the Chancellor would not want too many officials involved in any meeting, but I was determined to get the ones I trusted in there and not let Jonathan dominate. I didn't like the idea that there might be a row in front of the Chancellor – I knew he hated that.

The meeting with the Chancellor went ahead on schedule – something that took me off guard given the multitude of demands on his time. I knew that Sarah had told him that there was resistance to the idea among his advisers. But he hadn't used his old tactic of keeping the nay-sayers out of the key meeting. Clearly the Chancellor realised that whatever we did, this was a big move and he needed as much thinking and buy-in from his own team as he could manage. I had to take advantage of that if we were to come out with a decent way ahead.

We presented and he probed. Everyone was pretty well behaved given their views. Sunil gave the facts on the polling; I gave the facts on the analysis. Sarah, as so often in these bigger meetings, kept her counsel, much to my

97

annoyance. When Jonathan came to speak I tensed up and bit my pen rather hard. He was upbeat and positive, and the Chancellor smiled like a kid that hears a friend defend him in front of the teacher for something he should never have done.

As we talked through the issue, the Chancellor asked questions that showed he wasn't buying the majority steer to back off the whole thing – but was thinking of how to actually make it work. He wanted us to do more work, to see if we could find a way to overcome the problems we had identified. I feared he thought we were just blocking it out of some sort of spite that we had not invented the idea. I tried to keep cheerful, not letting him see that I thought this was a complete waste of our energies. I caught Sunil's eye and he shrugged. We knew there was further to go on this, whether we liked it or not.

Later that afternoon we met back in the office to consider what to do next.

It was a difficult meeting. All the tension that had been held back in the meeting with the main man could now be released. And it was.

"Well this is madness," began Sunil, leaning forward and getting things off his chest after having gone pretty softly in the Chancellor's meeting. That drove me up the wall – if he had been stronger then maybe the Chancellor would have come to his senses. But I knew that everyone was playing their own game in terms of their long run relationship with the Chancellor. "It's such a hard sell. Why does this government, that goes on about helping the poor, that put up taxes only two years ago to help pay for the NHS, now want to make a tax change that hardly helps the worst off? How the hell would we explain that?"

I was silently cheering Sunil on and the body language of the rest of the team showed I was not the only one. I wanted to come in behind him but was trying to keep neutral – especially as I did not know how this was going to go in the end. And I knew that Jonathan would have things to say.

"Come on, Sunil," Jonathan said, "I am sure you can come up with a convincing way of putting it that makes it feel consistent with our goals. You heard his argument: we need to show that we are not just instinctive tax raisers, or we will be easy prey for the Tories at the next election. It's the very counter-intuitive bits of these tax changes that work so well." He brushed his hands through his well-groomed hair. "Don't you agree, Sarah?"

I wanted to counter him, to point out that the detailed analysis showed that every way you cut this it looked a bad way of helping the people we claimed to be there for. But I bit my lip and pulled back. Jonathan was right; the Chancellor had heard all that but had stuck to his guns. Did I want to argue here in front of people who were closer to him than me, that he was just wrong?

While Sunil had his big doubts, I was almost certain he would not confront the Chancellor too strongly but just needed to get it all out of his system. So to the extent that any of them were, Sarah was my main ally on this one. She knew the Chancellor better than any of the rest of us, having worked for him from the years that he was in Opposition, fighting hard to get any airtime, giving unpopular messages to his colleagues about not making spending commitments everywhere. It had been a tough journey and Sarah had been with him on most of it. She knew that sometimes he did not do what was good for him. He needed to be stood up to at these moments – hard though that was and as angry as he sometimes got when questioned. And she was one of the few that could take that approach with him.

So it was a great relief when she decided to give her views. Everybody listened hard.

"I hear what you say, Jonathan. I don't think this is a great idea at all. And our political colleagues will ask what on earth we are doing when the teachers need more pay and when those who pay no income tax, the poorest, gain not a penny from this. I don't think No.10 will like it either so we will have another row at a time we just don't need it."

I smiled: Sarah was saying everything I wanted her to say. And the others – even Jonathan – were weighing up her words carefully: should they take their lead from her – or from him?

But then she tacked sideways.

"But the point the Chancellor is making is right: isn't it so, Sunil? We are thought of as the high tax guys and that could be very damaging electorally." Sunil nodded – albeit without enthusiasm. "So, if we don't like this idea, we need to find another one that works better to achieve that change in public perceptions."

My chin dropped and my cheeks sagged. I realised where this was now all going. I felt foolish, inexperienced, a failure. She was right of course. I had been focussing too much on showing why this idea, however you tried to finesse it, was the wrong way forward. But I had underplayed the importance of the politics: the need to change the story being told about us.

"Thanks, Sarah," I began, trying to feel my way forward and trying to sound confident about it. "So we are agreed that this is not the greatest idea but that we can't just knock it down – we need," I stumbled for the right way of putting it, "to find another way."

Jonathan banged his fist down on the table. "But there isn't one," he said angrily. "Maybe you guys can come up with something better – but I have tried and I can't. I think it does work. Just because the Chancellor invented it without discussing it with all of us first, does not make it a bad idea."

That really annoyed me and I gripped the edge of the table fiercely with both hands. *Bloody Jonathan and his City ways.* He was so used to getting his own way he was not prepared to listen to his colleagues who had been around far longer and were more battle hardened than he would ever be. I was furious. I half suspected that this whole stupid idea had come from Jonathan in the first place, meddling in an area he did not really understand.

But I needed to steady myself and I let my hold on the table loosen. I hadn't given up the aim of killing the whole stupid idea, but I knew that was not on – at least not yet. I took a risk.

"What do you think, Sarah?" I asked.

"Let's not give up on making this – or an alternative – work. In its current state it doesn't, but I am not convinced that it can't." That was enough for me.

"Okay" I said trying to get a grip once again. "Let's get on with two strands of work. One will be looking for an alternative approach to achieve the same goal the Chancellor is after. I'll work on that with Sunil. The other will be to see how we can best make it work if we do go down his path. I'll get officials to lead there but it will need help from everyone."

I spent the next few days desperately looking for some kind of alternative. I'd made that commitment and I felt pressure to come up with something. It was hard though – virtually impossible. Jonathan had been right on that one. My sleeping was getting increasingly bad and the migraines were starting to gather. I just could not work out what to do. If we went with what the Chancellor said he wanted I was sure it would be attacked and lose, not gain, us support– and anyway it was morally wrong. But how to get us out of this situation?

I had to find some time to talk to Sarah.

"I'm trying to find a way though this, Sarah, but it's difficult."

"Do you think there is a way through?" she replied icily. "Jonathan does."

"Jonathan is far too optimistic," I almost shouted. "How do you find a tax cut dramatic enough to change perceptions, but that doesn't end up giving a lot of money away to those who are not most in need?"

"You might be right," Sarah replied, "and we may have to get him there. But he won't like it"

"I know, I know, Sarah," I said despondently.

But it was more than despondence. I was angry now. This was not the time for tax cuts; our strategy should be to argue against those that advocated for them, not try to steal their clothes. It made me seethe that Sarah would not come off the fence some more and fully support that line. But I knew that she wouldn't – that she couldn't.

I tried other tacks too. I had to.

I got one of Chancellor's closer colleagues, an old friend, who occasionally helped out with speeches, to try and find a bit more about what was really going on in the Chancellor's mind. The report back didn't help me. The Chancellor was alarmed at letting the Party be painted into a tax and spend corner and wanted to shift the ground well before the next election. That trumped anything else.

I also managed to have a short, private conversation with the Chancellor. I played it carefully. Not, "This is madness!" but more of a "this is very challenging" tone. He listened – he was always polite to me – but nothing much changed.

The key meeting with the Chancellor was a few days later. I knew that I was in a losing position and I hated it. I was grumpy at home and short with my friends. Most of the rest of the team had switched from opposing to trying to make the policy as good as it could be – trying to reduce thresholds higher up the income range so that not too much of the benefit went to top rate taxpayers; adding in a package for those not paying tax; trying to limit the degree to which we actually raised the basic rate tax threshold. By the end this was a lot better and it was harder to be as opposed to it as I still wanted to be. But it didn't feel right – and letting Jonathan have his victory stuck in my craw.

The night before the meeting I struggled with how to play things. Over a large whiskey I sat alone, with the rest of the family fast asleep. As I swirled the dark liquid around in the glass, I went over and over things. I had made my points, done everything I could. Did I really want to continue the fight in this "public" arena before all my colleagues? Did I want to oppose a decision I knew was going to be made anyway? Question the judgement of a man whose instincts had so often turned out to be right to not only help us do good but also to help us win elections? Sometimes you had to take a step sideways, do something not really on your wish list at all, to be able to keep moving forward. It was a long game.

But to keep schtum when the whole policy made my gut churn was something I just could not do. Maybe I was less a political animal than I thought.

So, after a pretty sleepless night I, alone, argued one more time against going down this road. As I spoke, I could see my colleagues trying to avoid any eye contact with me or with the Chancellor. Those that I knew really agreed with me were the most awkward – Sunil, Sarah amongst them. But even Jonathan – who had proved the winner – clearly felt uncomfortable as I spoke. The Chancellor listened, thanked me, but firmly disagreed.

I let my hands drop to my sides and unhappy though I was, I felt a great weight lift from my shoulders. I had not bottled it in the name of peace and good relations. I had said what I should, and I could do no more. Now the decision was made, I could stop trying to change it.

But I had taken a big risk in taking this stance. I didn't know what impact it would have. It didn't change the policy – even if we'd ended up with a less troubling policy than the original, loose idea. But would it mean that I had lost all my influence with the Chancellor? Or, in the fast-moving world we worked in, would he forget and forgive? And what about the team I was leading; would they listen when they knew my view counted for very little in the final analysis? Or would they – and he – respect my desire to argue for what I thought was right?

Luckily, in the frenetic world of politics, there wasn't any time to dwell on that. We were quickly on to the next thing.

Demonstration

Peter's boss was a very decent woman indeed.

One of the most liked members of the Cabinet, Clare, the Secretary of State for Young People and Schools, was a natural on the Breakfast TV sofa, and popular even with some of the politicians on the other side. Indeed, the main criticism from her colleagues was that she wasn't political and tough enough.

But to the "DftK" she was the enemy. Big time. And they campaigned against her with everything they could throw. Because rightly or wrongly they believed that she was key to getting the government to support their agenda.

"Dads for their Kids" was originally a loose gathering of divorced fathers aggrieved at not getting enough access to their children. It had mushroomed into a substantial, but at times, anarchic group that thought direct action was the way to secure a law change. As Clare's special adviser, Peter had seen the way they had targeted Clare over the last year. They would gather outside the Department to protest so that coming to work you sometimes had to cross through lines of security guards keeping them at a distance. They would manage to get on to phone-ins or social media events whenever Clare was present. It was relentless.

Peter had tried a softly, softly tactic by offering them a meeting with himself. He had arranged for this to be over a coffee at a café near the office in Westminster, so the DftK did not have a chance for a dramatic protest outside the department.

Peter began.

"Look, the Secretary of State knows that you feel very strongly about this. But can we find some way of carrying forward this debate without it turning into a media circus?"

It was probably not the right thing to say.

105

"Do you have kids, Peter?" asked the leader of the group, a small man with a nice suit and a crisp, tie-less shirt. It was said quite softly with passion, but the aggression beneath the surface was clear.

"Yes, I do," Peter admitted. "I'm a dad alright." He had two young boys, but he wasn't going to give them that much detail.

"So, imagine you break up with your wife at some point and then the courts, and a judge who knows very little about you, says that you are hardly ever going to see your children again. That their mother gets more or less full custody. How does that feel, Peter?"

Peter did not want to be drawn into the rights or wrongs of their case. He also could not help wondering whether the judges might have been on to something with some of these men when they restricted access to their children. He knew he would never be in this position – and a picture of his family all together, with the boys laughing and mucking about and his arm around Josie his wife, came into his head. But so too did a picture of one of the recent rows he had had with Josie, something that was getting a bit more frequent. He put it down to tiredness and working too many late hours.

"I know it must be hard," he said. "As you know, we have a review of the law in this area going on and we will see what it comes up with." He meant that, but he also reckoned that the current law wasn't that awful. If the worst ever happened, he was sure no law would cut him off from his kids.

The leader stared Peter down. "It is not a media circus, Peter. It's our lives. And we will do whatever it takes." His words were said calmly but there was an unpleasant snarl on his face. "Just mark my words Peter. Just mark my words."

Peter reported all this back to his boss and at his suggestion Clare agreed to meet the group to try to take some of the heat out the situation. That did not go very well either. The meeting itself was as expected; they were angry and made their points with aggression. Clare had handled it pretty decently, being empathetic but giving no real ground.

But on the way out of the Department building the group skilfully chained themselves to an old statue of Gladstone in the reception area. Then, as the security guards came to take them away, another member of the team videoed the whole thing. For a rather chaotic campaigning group, they knew how to use everything they had. Soon it was up on social media and that evening he watched it on the late-night news as he sat on the sofa alone. Josie had already gone to bed and the boys were long tucked up in bed.

In the morning, he tried to talk to Josie about it all as she tried to get the boys ready for school.

"These men are maniacs, dangerous maniacs," Josie said sharply. "No wonder their wives wanted to get away from them and to hold onto the kids."

"Yes I know. But I do sort of understand their anger," he said but quite quietly so she probably didn't hear.

Not much changed over the next few months. They tried to ambush Clare a few times, but the security generally did its job. They also went for other ministers – with some media success. Meanwhile Josie had taken the kids away for a week to stay with her parents in the country. She'd said something about needing a break from him, but Peter didn't really hear that and anyway she was back now.

But now it was election time.

Lots of things changed during this period. Politicians wanted to be out meeting the public, speaking at meetings, pressing the flesh. Hiding was not an option. For those with a cause this was the period to really push hard and get your concerns debated by the parties and candidates. And on top of all this, the civil service ceased to be the guardians of the ministers during an election campaign – this fell much more to the Party organisations and the special advisers. In Clare's case, that meant Peter.

He and Clare – along with a couple of Party staff who helped organise election events – had met the police to talk about what the issues with "Dads for their Kids" might be.

"We know that these guys will be out to get publicity during the election campaign," said the policewoman in charge. "That is their right – as long as they do it peacefully."

"Will you be present at all our events to keep an eye and protect the Secretary of State?" asked Peter. He was concerned for Clare's welfare and he knew that Clare's husband was very anxious indeed.

"We will do our best – but we will be stretched during the campaign. You should have your own stewards at these things. And you have to keep your eyes open too; phone us if you suspect anything. Meanwhile, we will let you know if we pick up any intelligence about what they are up to."

"Do you have any intelligence at the moment?" Clare asked.

"Nothing specific. But we can be pretty sure they will try something at some point. We just hope it will be peaceful and harmless."

It was not that reassuring but there was not much Peter could do.

The campaign got going and Peter focussed on that. It was exhausting, exciting, non-stop, tense, and high pressure. He was hardly at home much in the hours that his boys were awake – leaving before they got up and returning home pretty late most nights. Josie had taken to making some pretty barbed comments about the kind of dad he was being. She had a point, but the need to win that election was paramount in Peter's mind. She would just have to put up with it.

Every now and then DftK did manage to capture the news. One of their members climbed Nelson's Column and unfurled a banner that said, "END THE WAR ON DECENT DADS" with a picture of a grieving child being torn away from its father. That got a bit of coverage in the news bulletins. But they were competing with lots of other election things and struggled to get that much publicity. And there were no attempts to ambush Clare.

After a while Peter stopped worrying so much and lost himself in the buzz that a general election campaign created. He did not travel with Clare around the country, being her "anchor" at Party HQ in London. He had two or three conversations a day with her when she was on the road, keeping her up to date on what was going on, briefing her on the tricky topics that were coming up, giving her space to let off steam about how things were going. He also spoke to the police every day to check if there was any news, and he spoke every other day or so to Clare's husband to take stock of where things were. Conversations about DftK slowly dropped down the list of things they discussed.

There was only a week to go before Election Day. The polls were tightening, and the opposition were doing well. The word went out to all Cabinet members to get out, be seen, ram home the Party messages. Clare was especially wanted to help get out the women's vote and up the profile of the Party policy on early years, nurseries, schools. Clare was a great message carrier and the campaign managers wanted more and more of her. It became frantic.

Peter was having to do a multitude of tasks: writing speeches for the events, helping with briefing before Clare's media appearances, answering questions from journalists on aspects of the Party's new curriculum policy, or its proposals on the early years' workforce, and liaising with the Treasury team about what they could say about how much any of this would cost and how they would pay for it. All this swirled around in his mind and the lack of sleep put it all into a blur. When the anxiety and adrenalin kept him awake at night he worried about not seeing much of his family, hardly seeing the boys, getting into silly, tired rows with Josie. It wasn't a good way to live. But the worst of it would be over soon.

The event Clare had been asked to do this Saturday was quite a big one. It was in London, so he was going to go to it. It was with a group of children's charities and Clare was going to launch one last pledge in this area – to do with guaranteeing more children's playgrounds. It had been a hard fight to get it agreed – even though Peter had had to be vague about the timetable and the scale to get it through the Treasury sift.

The venue was a reasonably large 1980's auditorium in a block next to a canal in North London. Peter was looking forward to seeing Clare live in action again – and kind of excited to see the TV cameras there too. He had done the police call that morning and they had not really added anything – in fact he felt they had got rather bored of the whole thing and seemed to be putting less and less effort into safeguarding Clare. But they did say they would be present which was a relief.

Clare was introduced by the Chair of the main children's charity that had been pushing for these playground changes.

Peter felt the nervousness he always had when he was listening to Clare say some of the words that he had written for her. Would it sound right? Had he got the tone right for the audience? Would it work on TV?

He was impressed with Clare. She must be much more tired than him, He knew she had missed seeing much of her young children over the last four or five weeks. But she was acing it – as ever. One day she would surely be the Party leader.

As Clare came to the point where she was to announce the new policy Peter felt everything jangling inside him. He could hardly bear to watch.

Then, without warning, two smartly dressed men from the second row got out of their seats and charged towards the podium. Before anyone could react, there was white powder being thrown at Clare. Peter's stomach churned – it could be anything, maybe it was anthrax powder.

Peter's thoughts went straight to Clare. Clare as a person, as his friend, as a mum and as a wife. That you could get killed for getting involved in politics was sickening and scary. What would he tell her husband who might well be watching, now, on TV? And how would his wife have felt if it had been him up there?

His mind moved fast on to actions. He had the urge to dash down from the back where he was sitting to try and help but it was all going too fast as two police officers rushed up towards the stage. It felt like they were going to catch the men before they got to Clare, but they could not get up onto the stage fast enough. By the time they had, one of the men, the one that Peter had spoken to back in that calm meeting at the café, had handcuffed himself to Clare and was screaming for everyone to keep away, threatening to do something unless his plea for Justice for Dads was heard. Nobody knew what to do. Was this a complete madman with intent to do damage to Clare?

Peter felt responsible. Why had he not noticed these men? For God's sake he had even met one of them before. Had he been paying enough attention to the safety issue instead of getting lost in what now seemed trivial bits of policy development? But why too had the police not seen this coming?

Most of the audience were being evacuated by the police. It seemed that the DftK brigade were just after what they already had – the shot on live TV that would be beamed out all over the place with accompanying packages about their cause and history. The white powder, the police assured Clare, was just flour. So, after a bit of talking to from the police the DftK men released Clare and took their arrest calmly.

Peter kept his distance. He was so wound up and angry that he did not trust himself. He wanted to go you up to the man he knew and shout in his face, "This is not a media circus. You have been playing games of terror with a woman's life."

He didn't – he knew it would achieve nothing. And anyway, the key thing was that Clare was OK.

One part of him wondered how some of these people slept at night. *How could you do that to anyone?* But another bit was conflicted. Somehow his involvement with these guys, crazy as they were, had made him feel just a bit of sympathy for them. If his wife walked out on him – and who would blame her after the last few months – might he end up in the same position as them?

He tiptoed back to his house quietly pretty late that night. He looked in on his wife in their bedroom, fast asleep and looking peaceful. He slowly went through the half open door of the boys' bedroom and stared at them for a few minutes. Then he went downstairs, sat down on the sofa, and he silently cried.

Empty Boxes

Jim walked more slowly than normal from Westminster Tube Station. Usually, he'd race down Parliament Street and Whitehall to make sure he got into work for the 7.30 morning catch-up meeting.

This morning there was no 7.30 meeting.

It was Jim's last day in No.10.

Technically it was his last day until after the election, but unless the opinion polls were lying very badly indeed, Jim would not be coming here again.

Jim tried to take it all in, to savour the experience, and yes the honour of having worked in such a place. The crisp but bright April weather cheered him, and the noise of the buses and the traffic felt familiar and friendly. He wanted to savour today not let himself descend into melancholy.

As he waited at the Downing Street gates, behind those trying to convince the police that they were on the official list for a meeting, he held up his pass and was waved in. Even dressed in jeans, shirt and sweater rather than the usual suit, he was recognised. He knew he would have been impressed watching someone pass through – and he wondered if the early morning tourists searching for a view of No.10 speculated as to who he was. What role he played. Or was that just the sort of thing only he would have wondered about?

No, the tourists probably did marvel at anyone who entered and exited. And at least he was something to wonder about as the chilly gaggle of tourists strained their eyes hoping to catch a glimpse of the Prime Minister.

Jim had always felt rather disorientated by the dichotomy between his government role and his normal life. When Jim got to work, he knew he was an important person helping make decisions that mattered. But he didn't really feel like that. He was just a normal guy, with, as far as he was concerned, no brilliant insights but just someone who had, through a variety of jobs and contacts, ended up with the skills and opportunity to get appointed to a job in No.10. His weekends were spent with his wife and kids, his mum and dad, a few of his friends. It was all very normal. But going into No.10 just wasn't.

The walk up Downing Street was a very public affair. The famous address was actually a short road blockaded at both ends by its big security gates. So once Jim had gone through the gates, he could just walk up the middle of the road – as long as no ministerial car was zooming up. But Jim almost never did that – it seemed not to be taking the place seriously enough. Today, as was his habit, he walked up the pavement on the opposite side from No.10 until he was more or less opposite the famous black, shiny front door. And then he crossed over. As was very often the case, there was no policeman outside the door and a short knock on the knocker was needed. He always felt a flutter of nerves at that moment; he saw his palms get a bit sweaty. Who was watching him? Was the whole world just waiting for him to screw up?

Then the door opened. And he smiled and enjoyed the feeling of awe, wonderment and nervousness. Jim never stopped marvelling at the perception that the interior of No.10 felt so much larger than the building appeared on the outside – a real life *Dr Who* Tardis. But it was also the thrill of the little boy about to enter Aladdin's Cave, or the hideout of one of the evil villains that James Bond had to track down; as though he was somewhere rather secret where he probably ought not to be.

Once behind the door, a massive world revealed itself inside this special place, bustling with energy, coupled with a certain degree of pomp and of historical constitutional significance, a world that he had somehow been allowed to enter.

Jim nodded in a familiar way to the smart, attentive No.10 guard ushering him in. Then all sorts of thoughts immediately clicked in – what he had to do that day, what meetings awaited him, how he would get it all done. But then he remembered with a jolt that there would be no meetings; he was only here to clean up and clear out.

Jim worked – as most No.10 Policy Unit staff did – in the main house that fronted Downing Street, away from the Cabinet and other "show" rooms that were further back. So after entering the building, he took a turn to the left and then went up an old staircase to his right. As he climbed the stairs, he realised with sadness that he was doing this probably for the last time and he couldn't help feeling nostalgic for the strange place. His hands, touching on the well-worn wooden banister for balance, were following the path of so many other hands over the centuries, some of them great, most forgotten; all of them part of history. Despite all the ancestry, this bit of Downing Street – out of public view, and with its old, underwhelming back staircase leading up to landings with a number of un-modernised rooms and corridors off them – could not help but remind him of a 1950's bed and breakfast: meaning well but stodgy, a bit naff, from an era before decent service really mattered. Two flights up he came to the landing where his office was, just a turn to the right at the top of the stairs.

Jim sensed a palpable quiet in the offices; the background hum of a place at work was all but absent. Jim wasn't surprised. Most of his "political" colleagues had already departed the building. Jim felt a bit awkward about that – staying behind to finish off government business while his former colleagues were out trying to win the election. On top of that, the civil servants could read opinion polls and so were preparing for a change of government and were finding it almost embarrassing to have relics of the old regime hanging around. Jim couldn't blame them but he felt unloved, untrusted, already an outsider to those who he had spent some years working with, being shunted, politely, away into the murky political world that civil servants disdained so much.

Jim opened the door, stopped and looked around. He took in the pretty ordinary, square room with a slightly sloping floor and a rather ropey brown carpet. Two desks sat diagonally opposite each other, both facing in. The one on the left was a standard, modern, if slightly scratched, maple-coloured office desk cleaned out as though by locusts; empty and already characterless. The person he had shared the office with had already cleared off and there was nothing left to suggest he had ever worked there. He could not help laughing at the sight of his own desk, over on the other side of the room, with a lot of junk on it – as ever. In addition, a whole load of his files and papers were stacked up next to his desk just as he had left them the day before. What was new in the room were about fifteen empty, cardboard boxes ready to be filled, balanced like children's blocks, on the floor in the middle of the room. Half neat, half messy, but whichever way Jim thought about it, "his" office was a rather sad and forlorn sight.

Jim looked at the dozens of books that he had taken from job to job… and now, again, they needed to be boxed up. Journals that had at times inspired him or that he had even written for. Books that followed and reflected his interests, covering things he had worked on over the years. Tomes that mapped out his life in different and not always obvious ways.

Quite a lot of the piles, Jim knew, consisted of copies of formal and official published government papers that he had been involved in. He picked one up and flicked through it: a technical government paper on the way to allocate the radio spectrum that lots of different businesses and bit of government wanted to get their hands on, something that probably only a couple of hundred people in the country knew or cared about. But, Jim reflected, an important paper that made it ultimately easier and cheaper for everybody's mobile phones to work. That one went in the "to keep" pile. Not all made that cut.

Another paper he thumbed through was about the government response to an EU proposal on the recycling of electrical products. Jim shrugged. It brought back memories of the debates about its content, but he nevertheless hurled it in the general direction of the bin. Definitely not one for filling up his shelves at home and annoying his wife with so much garbage. The same medicine was meted out to a green paper on reform of the Social Fund, the emergency fund that helped people in need when their cooker broke and they needed to buy a new one, a policy that had gone nowhere very fast, and he felt a touch of guilt for it having been so useless.

He found some good papers too, some that even now provoked a wave of pride within him – and some anger that the public looked poised to throw this government out. One was about making work-life balance a bit easier; another on a better way of regulating the utilities; still others on making coastal pathways open up to the public and on helping get more start-up finance available to entrepreneurs.

Then Jim turned his attention to the notes, the memos, the printed-out emails, all the material that was about internal debates, ideas, and disputes. Rather than the elegant piles of published papers, this set had been dumped down by the Downing Street staff in a heap, clearly a more or less clean sweep of what had been in his desk and filing cabinet.

He'd not kept much of this stuff since the Cabinet Office filing systems could produce old papers if you really needed it and because he had discovered through experience that he never did look much at old papers.

He sat in the middle of the room, very happy not to resist the lure of going through them.

They were a right old mix of things that – for one reason or another – he had held on to. Why had he kept all this? Maybe he was a bit mad, a compulsive hoarder unable to let go. Jim couldn't fathom what his criteria had been for deciding what would be kept and what would be shredded. What on earth was he going to find?

He explored deeper into the pile of papers. Some were individual papers; some were papers gathered together in transparent plastic folders. They were pretty random, kept by accident or laziness, the only criteria he could spot was where something had been a success – where he had clearly wanted to keep some sort of memento of them – or where it had niggled with him at the time.

He came across early drafts of speeches of the PM that he thought had gone well and the early musings of some policies – Jim guessed he had wanted to keep them to show he was in at the start. Some of this made him feel good, worthwhile, fulfilled. He had spent a good few years of his life working for this government and it made him feel like he had achieved something and made a positive difference to people's lives. But it wasn't all like that.

After a while, in an opaque blue folder, he found the beginnings of a government White Paper that never made it through. It was going to be about "Creating more good jobs", an admirable title and one that Jim recalled wryly the strategic communication guys were keen on as it would really chime with what the focus groups were saying. But as they'd drilled down into it, got some analysis done and brainstormed ideas, they realised they had very little to put in it that would lift if off the plate. Jim felt the pain reawaken. The basic ideas were worthy but dull, and the bold ones – like forcing employers to train their staff, to treat workers better – were rejected as too burdensome, too utopian to get a hearing.

Jim's passions were engaged. He looked up from his papers and stared at the reproduction of an impressionist painting hanging a bit askew on the wall.

Had that been the right decision? Was it just too cowardly or if not cowardly, then too governed by a view of what was possible and credible in the environment of the times?

Jim feared it was. And worse, it was him that had made that judgement and that made him feel ever so slightly sick. He remembered his conversation with Sue, his policy unit team member covering labour markets, trying to be firm and authoritative. "This just won't wash, Sue," he began, knowing he was doing everything he could to avoid eye contact. "And anyway, the employers would hate it and with all the other things we want them on-side for we can't afford to antagonise them by consulting on something we are never going to do anyway." He hesitated because he did not believe what he was about to say. "And which would probably not work even if we did do it." Jim wondered if Sue had realised how much he was pushing against his inner being as he refused to budge when she argued back. He squirmed at the memory, and he felt his stomach tighten up.

Another set of papers was about who was going to be given what job in the Cabinet when the new PM took office and what the PM wanted them to do in the department they were going to head up – papers Jim had worked on before they came into power. Now that was pretty secret stuff and

Jim was slightly surprised to see he had not shredded it. But he was pleased he hadn't as turning the pages of them brought a smile to his face. Not a smile of happiness but one of recognition at some old familiar issues that he had wrestled with once but had largely forgotten.

One of the biggest problems right at the beginning had been getting the right person in the right job, especially in the key Health portfolio. Originally Julia was pencilled in for Health. She had not been doing the job in opposition, but she was brilliant, energetic, different, and an ex-nurse to boot. She'd have taken no nonsense from the medics, but she also knew how to motivate them. Julia as Health Secretary would have given them all a lot of rocky days given her inexperience, but wow, Jim thought ruefully, what she might have achieved.

But Julia never was made Health Secretary. It went instead to the safe and perfectly fine Bill Sullivan. Jim recalled the sequence of events without much joy. Bill was originally offered the Transport job but he had kicked up big time. He said he would refuse the post, would prefer to go to the backbenches. The newly appointed Prime Minister panicked.

"Jim," he had asked, "can we really live with Bill leading the opposition against the government within the Party?"

Jim felt uncomfortable recalling how he had gone along with the PM's instinct. "Bill doing that would certainly cause us difficulties," he had begun. "Our majority looks OK but if Bill controlled twenty or thirty votes in Parliament – and he could – then every issue would become a negotiation."

"So what do we offer him?" Deborah, the PM's long term personal assistant, had asked.

"He wants one of the big jobs. Home Office, Treasury,

Foreign Office. But I can't be seen to reward Bill that much or I'll lose face," the PM had commented with a shake of his head.

"It has to be one of the next ones down then," Jim had chipped in, looking for a way out.

"I reckon Health would buy him off," said Deborah.

"But hang on," Jim had replied, realising the implications of where this logic was taking him. "Bill is great in some things, but health? We have such good plans to make it much more focussed on patients and Julia will be terrific and Bill... well Bill will always side with the docs and the unions."

"It's not what we wanted," Deborah had agreed, "but what else do we do? We've got to get this Cabinet sorted out now. The press are already speculating on why the delays. So it's Health or he goes and disrupts your whole premiership, Prime Minister."

It had been a conclusive argument. So Bill had become Health Secretary and many dreams and hopes had thereby gone by the board. Maybe it had all worked OK – politically at least. Health was still one of the strongest suits the government had, and the public still seemed to like what they had been doing. But in one moment of cowardice – or *realpolitik,* as Jim preferred to think of it – out went all the ideas and plans Jim had always dreamed of implementing, and that he thought were needed to really improve the health system.

Not all the papers were that interesting. Jim uncovered memos to the PM about the timing of various announcements on flood defence; a whole set of analyses and increasingly intemperate e-mails looking at the interminable issue of the fairness of how much public spending Scotland got in support relative to England; and even, for some reason he could no longer recall, papers about the visit of an obscure South American leader. These got a cursory glance before going in the "to shred" pile. He spent a bit more time looking through some incongruous papers that he'd kept for some reason he no longer understood, about some maintenance work needed to the Downing Street building, debating where his staff would be re-housed for the duration. Typical, that despite all that effort the works never actually happened. Those papers he threw on the chuck pile too.

Then Jim found the PowerPoint slides outlining how the new regime might re-engineer the centre of government and that really did get his juices going. It had been about a year into Howard Peters' premiership and Jim remembered it clearly. Things were not going too well. Tensions within No.10 were simmering – as they always were when the opinion polls took a nosedive. The Treasury seemed to be doing their own thing, as though they were not part of the same government. And plotting and gossip seemed to be on a sharp incline.

So the Prime Minister's inner team – with Jim a key member – had put their minds to trying to think about ways of working that might bring more of the Cabinet into decision making, ways to get No.10 and the Treasury to work closer together so there was collective buy-in to a unified strategy and work programme.

The ideas had been presented to the PM and he liked them. So next, it was to be presented to Doug, the Chancellor of the Exchequer, the boss of the Treasury and the effective "Number 2" in the government. If he was on side it all had a chance of taking off and working.

The PM was nervous, however. And with good reason.

"I want to take Doug through this carefully and privately," he told Jim. "This is about creating a stronger government but if we do this wrong Doug will see it as an attempt to clip his

122

wings and he will react pretty badly." He looked Jim straight in the eye. "So I don't want anyone in our team talking to anyone about this. Anyone."

But things got tricky. Jim had to take a call from Doug's special adviser when he rang through, asking why the Chancellor had suddenly been invited over for a private one-to-one. If he did not know, he had said, then Doug was not going anywhere. The adviser's attitude and tone on the call made Jim's blood boil, but it was a fair request. Any decent spad, as Special Advisers were generally known in the Whitehall world, would want to make sure their boss was not ambushed, and knew what was going on.

But Jim made a mistake, one that still made his guts churn all this time later: he sent the draft paper to Doug's spad. And while he did not altogether blame his opposite number, the next thing he knew, the press were on to the story. The whole thing had quickly spiralled into a No.10 versus Treasury argument, the most dangerous type for any government. Doug was furious and No.10 had to ditch all the ideas for change and so the difficult and often debilitating relationship with the Treasury not only carried on but got worse.

Jim put these papers in a pile to take home to keep. He wanted to keep them because though it made him cringe and shake his head, it had been a lesson and he did learn from it, becoming more circumspect, understanding better the way that politics at this level really worked. But Jim knew deep down that it was a sort of sad coming of age and a growing up – an acceptance of a degree of caution even when dealing with your "trusted" colleagues.

Jim stared out of the window. Now all he could see was the side wall of the building across Downing Street, with its arch into the Foreign Office next to it and the empty Downing Street below. It was not always like that though.

Sometimes when there was a really big event going on in Downing Street there were dozens or even hundreds of journalists outside the building. When the US President came they even built a special stand so the journos and snappers could all get a view.

Now that was something surreal. Jim remembered with a strange mix of pride and amusement watching the TV in his office showing "live" the view from the same cameras he was looking at out of his window. What a gas! He wanted to phone someone to tell them, or to somehow record the event. But a few blurred pictures on his phone did not quite tell the tale. He recalled wondering if the cameramen and journalists outside might look up and catch a glimpse of him watching them on TV watching him. Surreal indeed.

What an honour to have worked here. What a dream.

And now it was at an end. And did those papers and memories say: "Well done, Jim, you did a good job"? Or did they in fact say, "What, was that all you did?"

Jim had always worried about that verdict of history issue even though he knew that no historian would be writing about "The role of Jim in British politics – was he any good?" That verdict would, of course, be produced in relation to his boss and Jim would get some footnote in that – if anything at all. After all, the job of special advisers was to serve not to be the story.

But at a personal level he had so much wanted to do his best when he arrived in this job. He had believed for so many years that if the Party could only be in government, it could make a real difference to people's lives and he had always hoped that he could have a role in making that happen. When he had secured a job, the job he had dreamed about doing, he had felt he must not fail. Being mediocre, doing OK and not screwing up was important, but he had wanted to do so much more than that.

He used to moan about his predicament to his wife. It wasn't always the easiest conversation as she already thought he gave too much of himself to the job relative to ever seeing his family or spending decent time with her.

A moan went something like this:

"I was pretty useless at work today."

"What do you mean?" asked Cathy, at least a little sympathy in her tone. "Did something go badly wrong?"

"Not really badly," Jim replied, "but something that I've failed on."

"Sure it is all your fault?"

"Well, something I'd been pitching for ages collapsed today. And I should have been able to do better. I just should have managed it so much better."

"Don't beat yourself up about it too much," Cathy said although Jim could sense that the sympathy was fading away – after all it was just a normal day at the office, "we all get things wrong."

She paused, but clearly sensing that Jim wanted a bit more, she gave him another prompt. "So, why didn't you manage to get it through?"

"Why didn't I?" echoed Jim. "That is exactly the question, Cathy. Why didn't I succeed? What did I do wrong?"

That question was one that haunted him a great deal on many issues over his time in government. He had tried, but he knew he had not always got it right. As a special adviser, he was there to help out the elected politicians. To advise them, to be of support, to do the politics that civil servants could not and should not do, to explain to others what the politicians wanted. But Jim was certain that he had to do more than that. You weren't only there to do what the politicians thought of. but to help them think, to help them overcome obstacles, to help them deliver what was right. And if Jim could not do that, what was the point?

But in so many cases a great idea, a new bold initiative, never went anywhere. They died and the moment was gone. Jim looked at the boxes around him in his old room, looked around the office, and shook his head just a little. It was late afternoon now and the Spring sun was a lot lower in the sky. Was that the real lesson from his years so close to power – that it is all a joke? That nobody is out to make the world better but just to survive and not screw up? Was that in fact his real epitaph?

Jim went back to the boxes. There was some good stuff there. Many were attempts to do good things – but only attempts for Christ's sake. He came across papers describing a way to get the country and world moving on climate change, but never the move to a serious carbon tax that might have really helped. He knew why: too difficult.

He found papers from early in the regime all about constitutional change – he had somehow got involved in that despite not knowing too much about it – which led to some useful change around reducing the old, traditional royal prerogative in areas. But the big stuff – Lords reform, voting reform – all untouchable.

The papers were all sorted and the boxes were taped down. His name was clearly labelled on each. They were going to be picked up and delivered to his home. Jim went downstairs slowly, said goodbye to the policeman on the door, left the building and walked back up Downing Street to the big entry gates to re-join the normal world outside. He knew this would be the last time he would do that. His mood was low, his head down.

He didn't take the Tube but went for the bus instead. He couldn't bear to be underground, packed up against all the commuters. He did not often take the bus and usually when he did, he was glued to his mobile or was flicking through various papers. This time he stared out of the window.

And strangely on this trip he noticed things he did not always notice. A school with new buildings and what looked like a redone playground. Council houses with notices saying that they had received investment to do them up, mend the windows, put in new lifts and security measures, and to modernise the kitchens. Round one corner he glimpsed a new children's centre with bright, happy mosaics outside. Jim felt a sense of pride as well as anger. And he felt his eyes water and his throat tighten.

It maybe wasn't as much as he'd dreamed of, but he knew it was something. Maybe some of it was worth it after all.

About the Author

Dan Corry wrote many short stories in his twenties – and had one published as a result of a competition in a PEN New Writing collection (edited by Alan Massie).

After that his writing energy mostly went into writing reports, speeches and White Papers, as well as newspaper articles as he worked in think tanks and then as a special adviser during most of the Labour government 1997-2010. An economist by profession, he worked in various departments including Business, Education, Treasury and Downing Street. He now runs a charity that seeks to improve the impact of that sector.

Only in the last few years has he taken up short story writing again. And he is enjoying it! He had a short story published, *Running the Line – Fairlight* but this is his first collection of short stories. He lives in South London and tries to play a bit of jazz saxophone.

Acknowledgements

Many thanks to all who I worked for and with as a special adviser. It was a privilege and mostly a joy. Thanks to Debz Hobbs-Wyatt who helped me make the stories be a bit more "show than tell" and to Laura Peters who first thought that these stories had something in them and helped me in the early editing of one of them. And of course, thanks to my family who saw rather little of me during my spad years – Dinah, Elsa and Joe.

Like to Read More Work Like This?

Then sign up to our mailing list and download our free collection of short stories, *Magnetism*. Sign up now to receive this free e-book and also to find out about all of our new publications and offers.

Sign up here:
    http://eepurl.com/gbpdVz

Please Leave a Review

Reviews are so important to writers. Please take the time to review this book. A couple of lines is fine.

Reviews help the book to become more visible to buyers. Retailers will promote books with multiple reviews.

This in turn helps us to sell more books... And then we can afford to publish more books like this one.

Leaving a review is very easy.

Go to https://amzn.to/46Ru0Fp, scroll down the left-hand side of the Amazon page and click on the 'Write a customer review' button.

Other Publications by Bridge House

The Story Weaver
by Sally Zigmond

Story-telling has often been associated with weaving and
spinning. All is craft, cleverness and magic.

Here indeed we have a colourful mix of beautifully crafted
stories. Some are sad and others bring us hope. There are
tensions in relationships, fear of the unknown coupled with
surprising empathy, and accidents of birth. Death wishes are
reversed, sometimes but not always, and so are lives in other
realties. People's stories intersect as they wait for a bus. An old
cello causes havoc. A church clock always strikes twice… or
does it? Match-making goes wrong until it goes right. And so
much more.

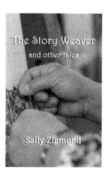

"A wonderful collection of interesting tales. A real mixture
that will delight all readers." *(Amazon)*

Order from Amazon:

Paperback: ISBN 978-1-914199-54-7
eBook: ISBN 978-1-914199-55-4

The Adventures of Iris and Zach
by I.L. Green

Iris and Zach have an uneasy but intriguing run.

A vast patchwork landscape of life is displayed through stories relating both the wonder and absurdity we all recognize. With a focus on mental health, these stories take the reader from incarceration to freedom, fear to comfort. There are celebrations of life and poetic lows. The Yin and Yang aspects of life are recognized in new and deliberate examples that instil thoughtfulness and occasionally a smile.

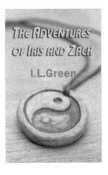

Order from Amazon:

Paperback: ISBN 978-1-914199-34-9
eBook: ISBN 978-1-914199-35-6

A Gentle Nudge
by Mason Bushell

Stories to soothe your soul.

In a world drowning in negativity and dark events, we all need a little light and hope. With a little adventure, romance and even music, these short stories will give your hopes and dreams a nudge as they draw a smile.

A Gentle Nudge by Mason Bushell wraps you in calm.

Order from Amazon:

Paperback: ISBN 978-1-914199-42-4
eBook: ISBN 978-1-914199-43-1